ANTHONY BOURDAIN

ANTHONY BOURDAIN
THE LAST INTERVIEW
and OTHER CONVERSATIONS

with an introduction by HELEN ROSNER

MELVILLE HOUSE
BROOKLYN · LONDON

ANTHONY BOURDAIN: THE LAST INTERVIEW AND OTHER CONVERSATIONS

Copyright © 2019 by Melville House Publishing
First Melville House printing: August 2019

"Cooking Up a Mystery: An Interview with Anthony Bourdain" © 2003 by Jessica Bennett. First published in *Rain Taxi Review of Books* in Summer 2003.

"Medium Raw: In Conversation with Anthony Bourdain." © 2011 by Jill Dupleix. Presented by The Sydney Writers' Festival on May 21, 2011.

"Anthony Bourdain Dishes on Food." © 2013 by Neil deGrasse Tyson. First appeared on *Star Talk with Neil deGrasse Tyson* on April 7, 2013.

"Anthony Bourdain Talks Travel, Food, and War." © 2014 by John W. Little. First published on Blogs of War on July 20, 2014.

"Anthony Bourdain on Food: There's Nothing More Political." © 2016 by Canadian Broadcasting Corporation. First appeared on CBS News' *On the Money* with Peter Armstrong on November 7, 2016. Used with permission from CBC Licensing.

"Telling Stories Through Food on 'Parts Unknown.'" © 2018 by Viacom. First appeared on Comedy Central's *The Daily Show with Trevor Noah* on January 17, 2018.

"The Last Interview: Anthony Bourdain on Asia Argento, His Favorite Movies, and Why Trump Would Be a Terrible Dinner Companion." © 2018 by Penske Media Corporation. First published on IndieWire on June 3rd, 2018. Used with permission from Wright's Media as agent for Penske Media Corporation.

Melville House Publishing   Suite 2000
        46 John Street   and   16/18 Woodford Road
        Brooklyn, NY 11201   London E7 0HA

mhpbooks.com
@melvillehouse

ISBN: 978-1-61219-824-8
ISBN: 978-1-61219-825-5 (EBOOK)

Printed in the United States of America

3   5   7   9   10   8   6   4
A catalog record for this book is available from the Library of Congress.

CONTENTS

INTRODUCTION

HELEN ROSNER

Right after high school, I spent an entire summer staring at Anthony Bourdain's face. After graduation, I had wrangled a job at the Seminary Co-op Bookstore in Chicago, where I spent thirty hours a week ringing up customers at a hiccupy, green-screen register terminal. For me, the summer was a prairie stretching out into hazy infinity; I was leaving for college at the end of it, but ten weeks may as well have been a hundred years. The bookstore was serious and scholarly, independent but affiliated with a major university, and it was strictly stocked: no kids' books, no cookbooks, no travel, no genre fiction. Our inventory's few concessions to a buyer's impulse to make impulse buys lived by the register, piled in a few short stacks, their spines becoming as familiar to me as the back of a crush's neck. I don't know how trustworthy my memory is anymore, but I remember ringing up a copy of *Kitchen Confidential*, Bourdain's just-published memoir and that summer's runaway hit, every fourth or fifth customer— locking eyes a half a dozen times an hour with the white-clad, knife-holding author on the cover, his sharp cheeks and pursed lips framing a Mona Lisa glare.

Store employees weren't technically supposed to read on the job, but what else was there to do? I worked my way through Bourdain's book in bites and gulps over the course of a week, reading half a chapter until a customer arrived, then selling them the copy in my hand. Did reading *Kitchen Confidential* change my life? Hard to say. I was nineteen, soft-handed, drowning in my own wishes and terrors, a kitten with its eyes still closed. What could I have believed about fancy restaurants, that this book upended my notions of their sanctity? What could I have known about food writing that it shattered my sense of its limits?

The book did, of course, change everything—for restaurant-goers and for writers, and most powerfully, for cooks, who were, in a single instant, as if from on high, deliv-ered a spokesman, and champion, and poet laureate. It also explosively changed everything for Bourdain himself. He was 44 years old when *Kitchen Confidential* was published, and he thought of this memoir as an endcap to his career: a way to stuff and mount those bone-splintering years spent work-ing the line, wringing some value (literary, monetary) from his lost years, his time as a junkie and then getting clean, the splendor and indignity of a cook's jagged life. The book's more practical secret-spilling quickly took on the patina of conventional wisdom—everyone, it seems, now knows not to order fish on Mondays, and to steer clear of the refrigerator dumping ground of an off-menu frittata special, even if they don't always know where that knowledge came from.

Readers may have bought the book to get insight into a world ten feet from their dinner table, but it was Bourdain the man who kept us reading—the character on the page, the voice recounting the story. To me, a teenager in a half-slouch behind the counter at the bookstore, each page was an astonishment: raunchy and vicious and wild, all of it in prose sharp as a scimitar. Bourdain is best known, now, for his extraordinary television career, and he's most often categorized as a cook, but to me he's always a writer—he's the author of some dozen books, and uncountable essays and blog posts and show notes—and *Kitchen Confidential* is the knuckle-crack of a fighter getting ready to wallop. I still catch my breath reading his description of the palms of a fearsome chef, a line that wouldn't be out of place in *Moby-Dick*: "The hideous constellation of water-filled blisters, angry red welts from grill marks, the old scars, the raw flesh where steam or hot fat had made the skin simply roll off."

• • •

Despite my love affair with *Kitchen Confidential*, I didn't read another Bourdain book until around 2014, after deciding that I probably ought to understand why this Bourdain guy was still such a big deal. Like most former teenaged bookstore employees, I'd figured that one day I'd end up being a writer, but it had been something of a surprise that I'd ended up writing about food and restaurants. Still, some contrary impulse in me refused to engage even a little with Bourdain's career, assuming—based on his omnipresence, his tremendous success, and his universal belovedness, not to mention that he was all anyone talked about when we talked, endlessly, about bad-boy tattooed chefs and their rock-star lives—that he was probably an overrated hack.

I started with *Medium Raw*, the putative sequel to *Kitchen Confidential*, published ten years later and being, more or less, a meditation on the wild fame that followed the first book's publication. He had me from the first line: "I was so supremely naive about so many things when I wrote *Kitchen Confidential*," the book begins, then runs in a stream of consciousness from chapter to chapter: marveling at the absurdities of private air travel, eviscerating the sanctimony of Alice Waters, exploring the strange sensuality of writing about food, grappling with his conflicting feelings about still being called "chef" despite not, technically speaking, being the chief of anyone anymore. He writes about being recognized by a young cook at a bar: "'Fuck you,' he says. 'You don't even cook. You're not one of us anymore.' Far from being offended (though I am hurt), I want to give him a big hug. Another drink or two, and I just might."

What I hadn't realized before reading *Medium Raw* was that Bourdain had written it as a corrective. The bro-chef culture that *Kitchen Confidential* had illuminated and invigorated had metastasized way beyond Bourdain's comfort zone—he was already done with life as a cocky, drug-addled cowboy by the time *Kitchen Confidential* was published, but to some of his readers, it would always be written in the present tense. To his great discomfort, wherever he went, young cooks would offer to get high with him, or brag about screwing their co-workers during service, or stealing cash, or doing unspeakable things to the produce inventory. *Medium Raw* is an uneven book, a collection of ideas and memories—some sections read like outtakes from *Kitchen Confidential*—but its best moments are among Bourdain's most indelible work. But by the time it came out, in 2010, Bourdain's television celebrity was so massive that another book—even one dishing on all the T.V. secrets—was pretty much just a radar blip.

The shows, when I tracked them down in reruns, were even better. From the beginning, in the Food Network show *A Cook's Tour*, which began production just a few months after *Kitchen Confidential* hit shelves, Bourdain's voice was true. In the early days you can see how much he wanted to make sure we knew he was cool; as he eased into his on-camera self over the years, you can almost watch the affect falling away, the posture of cynical indifference giving way to more of a nihilist delight.

After two years with the Food Network, Bourdain launched a new show with the Travel Channel, *No Reservations*—a bigger, smarter, more idiosyncratic eating-around-the-world show. This eventually led to a deal with CNN, where Bourdain and his team produced what is likely the pinnacle of the travel form. *Anthony Bourdain: Parts Unknown* was ostensibly a food show, but it's more accurate to think of it as a brutally beautiful documentary series, or a ballistic missile of pure humanity, a meticulous and often radically compassionate exploration of not only what people eat around the world, but the deep and indelible why: the wars, the zoning

laws, the climate disasters, the religious strife, the histori-
cal necessity. He went to beautiful, vacation-ready locations,
but also filmed powerful and humanizing episodes in places
that to most of his viewers exist only in clichés of violence
and poverty: Iran, Gaza, Congo, Madagascar, Libya, Cuba.
Bourdain also made a point to turn the camera on America,
and to give it the same unsparing combination of love and
scrutiny that he brought everywhere else. "Like any other
episode of *Parts Unknown*, whether in Vietnam or Nigeria or
any city in the United States, this West Virginia episode is a
plea for understanding of the people whose personal histo-
ries, sense of pride, independence, and daunting challenges
deserve respect," he wrote in his show notes for an episode
unpacking the clichés of coal country. "It's a walk in somebody else's shoes."

• • •

When Bourdain died, in 2018, it felt like the world was
knocked off course. Death is always a shock, even when we
see it coming, even if we've been watching it creep towards
us all the way from the horizon. But Bourdain's suicide was
sudden, unfathomable. It felt like a mistake: surely it wasn't
him, surely it wasn't real. It has been difficult for me to try to
separate the sorrow of losing my friend Tony from the sorrow
of losing Anthony Bourdain, Public Figure. But the more I
try to disentangle them, the more I begin to feel that there
may not actually be all that much to disentangle.

    At the news of his death, millions of people mourned

—and not the way that we mourn a commodity celebrity, with a sharp breath of sorrow and a fleeting salute and a sad-face post on social media. Millions of people mourned Bourdain the way you mourn a friend: primal, personal, disbelieving, unreal, unhealed. The astronaut Scott Kelly, former commander of the International Space Station, wrote of Bourdain, "Following his travels while I was in space brought me home to our planet. He made me feel like I was walking barefoot over those places that were so far below. For a moment, while I watched his show, I felt a little bit like I was back on Earth, sticking my toes in the water of life."

Being part of that great global outpouring of sorrow was unlike any public death I have ever experienced—a feeling of being unexpectedly untethered and left to drift, entirely alone, all together. The impact of his loss rippled outward for days, weeks, months—even now, it's still raw, the space he left is still a gaping emptiness. The senselessness of his death is somehow more enormous, still, than the great work of his life. This will ease over time, I know: the open wound will close into a scar, the scar will fade into the crosshatched dullness of memory.

Most celebrities in the culinary world fit one category or another: you can loosely bundle together your domestic goddesses, your reality-tv judges, your globe-trotting trend-seekers, your toffee-nosed haute cuisine auteurs, all of them individually distinct but speaking, culturally, at comparable pitch and volume. Bourdain defied category, which means he defies replacement. There's no other ex-line-cook memoirist, who's also an advocate for culinary justice, who also makes the best goddamn show on television, who also has the ear of global leaders, who also reads a hundred books a year and

xiv   Introduction

knows every film ever made, and has the irresistible charisma
of a black hole, and writes like a burning knife, and wears his
anger and his sadness on the outside, right next to his delight.
When he died, he was at the pinnacle of his career, riding a
wave of professional and creative fecundity, by most measures
deeply fulfilled in his personal relationships. He'd sent me a
note a few days before, a flutter of empty and delicious gos-
sip, and had then sent another when I didn't answer quickly
enough for his liking. In the days after he died, I stared at that
last message in my inbox, the sarcastic demand for a reply, an
unanswerable question.

•   •   •

Coincidentally, it was right in the middle of my self-imposed
Bourdain immersion course that I met him—the real him,
not the textually intermediated version of him—for the first
time. This was where I ran into my Tony problem. Even after we became friends, I had a hard time calling Bourdain
"Tony." He would tease me about it, and speculate about
which presumably deep Freudian well my resistance to his
preferred name sprang from. "It's because you take an intense
professional interest in me," he suggested, once, as an explana-
tion, which I suspect came close to the truth — in print, he's
always Anthony Bourdain, no matter how much he's Tony at
home. And, maybe because of my self-imposed late exposure
to his works, the particular nature of my professional interest was not about the substance of his career—the first time
I formally interviewed him, a ninety-minute conversation

recorded for the podcast the *Eater Upsell*, I admitted with embarrassment that I still had never seen any episodes of *Parts Unknown*—but instead about its form.

Bourdain seemed to me to be a fascinating specimen of celebrity. He was one of the best-known people in America, and possibly in the world, a notoriety on par with heads of state and Hollywood superstars, but his life lacked any of the insulation that normally comes with such a profile. He didn't walk through Manhattan with a security detail, or insist on photo approval, or barricade himself behind a battalion of publicists. The most striking thing to me was the closeness his fans felt to him—a genuine sense of friendship and communion, a sense of comfort with his intimate self. A few years ago I had coffee with a college student who wanted my advice on becoming a food writer. I asked him whose work he admired, and he didn't even need a last name: "Tony, of course."

Undoubtedly, part of Bourdain's everyman appeal came from the fact that he was a prolific interviewee; journalists reaching out to him—usually by way of an email to his collaborator (and self-described gatekeeper) Laurie Woolever— were almost never met with a "no," and the conversations in this volume are just a sliver of the vast public archive of his commentary. Here, he is his true, dynamic self, cranky and smart and utterly charming. But what's most evident to me, in these particular selections, is how hard Bourdain fought against the flattening effects of fame, how urgent it was for him, always, to be a full and multidimensional person even in his public self—to have space to evolve in his craft, to inhabit new perspectives and priorities. He politely answers the same questions over and over, gently steering the conversation into the present: breezing past the drugs and crime and horrors of brunch, gently pointing out that he doesn't really do the cobra-blood shtick anymore, pivoting to the eye-opening effects of fatherhood, the demands of creativity, the moral obligations of success and the illuminating benefits of being a professional curious outsider. "I used to think that basically, the whole world, that all humanity were basically bastards," he tells John W. Little, in a 2014 interview for *Blogs of War*. "I've since found that most people seem to be pretty nice— basically good people doing the best they can."

These interviews trace the arc of just fifteen years, from his early fame to shortly before the end of his life. Maybe it's because Bourdain spent more adult years as a civilian than a celebrity, but the man talking about his hustler's work ethic in the *Rain Taxi Review of Books* in 2003 is the same person leaning back in his chair in 2018, chatting with Trevor Noah in front of the cameras of the *Daily Show* about his rage at the President of the United States referring to El Salvador, Haiti, and the entire continent of Africa as "shithole countries." There's maybe a little more comfort, a little more authoritative confidence, a little more weariness in the voice. But he was, from the start to the finish, exactly himself. It was all there in *Kitchen Confidential*, if you go back, and you know what to read for: the story of a man looking for himself, going for glory, fucking up, and winning big, the whole time never quite sure if getting caught and getting away with it hadn't actually been the same thing all along.

ANTHONY BOURDAIN

COOKING UP A MYSTERY: AN INTERVIEW WITH ANTHONY BOURDAIN

INTERVIEW WITH JESSICA BENNETT
RAIN TAXI REVIEW OF BOOKS
SUMMER, 2003

Anthony Bourdain has come a long way since the release of his first two mystery novels, *Bone in the Throat* and *Gone Bamboo*. His curriculum vitae now contains two hit non-fiction books (*Kitchen Confidential* and *A Cook's Tour*) and the television show *A Cook's Tour*, which, with the possible exception of *Iron Chef*, is the best show on the Food Network. Bourdain's following includes fellow chefs and restaurant workers, as well as those of us outside the industry who admire their outlaw lifestyle and love good food.

Bourdain's latest book, *The Bobby Gold Stories*, is a short collection of self-contained stories about a New York mafia tough-guy, and Nikki, the sexy sous-chef he falls in love with. The disparate stories add up to a crime novel that's a comedic page-turner. I talked with Bourdain in Minneapolis about fiction, food, and a few other sizzling topics during his recent book tour.

JESSICA BENNETT: Do you consider *The Bobby Gold Stories* to be, at heart, a love story?

BOURDAIN: Well, it is kind of a love story, a dysfunctional love story. I didn't know that I was writing one at the time. I'd been writing about myself for two books, talking about myself on television, and frankly I'm bored with the subject. Maybe I'm working through some personal issues here. I was also very much under the influence of the Pat Hobby stories by Fitzgerald. Not that I write anything like Fitzgerald, but he wrote these stories when he was at his abject lowest point in his career, all about a failed screenwriter named Pat Hobby. He wrote them to put his daughter through Vassar and sold them to magazines. And when they were published in a collection it was this lovely sequence of long short stories, all with the same character, and all of them, at least putatively, in order. And I thought, wow, that's a really fun thing to do, they can both stand alone and have some sense of continuity. I just wanted to enjoy myself, and I didn't want to have to chase my characters up a tree, the denouement—I don't care who done it in crime books or why they done it, I care what they're wearing, what the room smells like, what's cooking, that sort of thing. I think those things speak volumes about people.

BENNETT: And what they're listening to as well.

BOURDAIN: What they're listening to. The record collection, always very important.

BENNETT: I notice that you mention the Modern Lovers in at least a couple of places, which thrills me to no end, because I think Jonathan Richman is a genius.

BOURDAIN: You know his greatest album, he hates—the first record, *The Modern Lovers*. He won't perform it. I love "Someone I Care About." There's this great line,

There's a certain kind of girl
That you care about so much
I don't care what you guys do to me
but her, don't touch.

It's just a guilelessly wonderful song. I'm a huge fan of that album, that mixture of naiveté and earnestness and cynicism and everything else.

BENNETT: There's also this concern there for the people around him, for people who are destroying their lives, in a similar way to how the people in your books are sometimes destroying their lives—especially with the biggie, drugs.

BOURDAIN: Yeah, well, it's very autobiographical. I deliberately set out to make my hero and heroine as unsympathetic as I could possibly make them and yet still make you want to keep reading. I don't know whether I pulled that off, but to me, it's not will they get the bad guy, or will they get away with it; what interests me when I'm reading is whether I'm still going to like this guy next chapter. That issue is seriously in doubt in *The Bobby Gold Stories*. And I always try to find a way to like the bad guy a little bit.

Bobby is a little guy in a big body. He's bulked up to this monster size, but he's basically a pussycat. He's shy, he's socially inept. I guess it's kind of a parable for what you become when you become a chef. Also, this book is very much a reflection of . . . you know, I got health insurance for the first time a couple of years ago, after I wrote *Kitchen Confidential*, and I had my walls painted for the first time, and I bought a little furniture. And I was just so giddy to be doing something normal. I'd lived on the fringes, paycheck to paycheck, for 28 years, and I'd always been curious about the massive, abstract entity out there in the dining room. What was it like to own a home, have a lawn, own a car, have kids, any of those things. So it's about two people who have their nose pressed against the glass, but who in their own weird, dysfunctional way are trying to emulate Beaver Cleaver.

BENNETT: It's a natural fit for Bobby and Nikki to end up together, Bobby the gangster and Nikki the cook.

BOURDAIN: I think so. She made herself into this rough, tough, heavily armored character and so did he. They both want something, and in their own, inept way, they're looking to play house.

BENNETT: There are places in your fiction where you write voraciously about food, and the other place where I see that kind of passion is in the sex in the books. There seems to be this really strong connection between food and sex in both your fiction and non-fiction.

BOURDAIN: Taking pleasure in food has always been associated with sin. Food and sex have been closely aligned in the

Judeo-Christian ethic going right back to the very beginning and the apple. If you don't like sex, if you don't like music or movies, chances are you're not eating well, either. Yes, I think there's a close connection personality-wise, but also physiologically, you undergo many of the same physiological changes in anticipation of a good meal as you do with sex. I think they're closely aligned. I read a lot of food writers, and I'm always thinking, this person writes about food like they've never had good sex in their life. I think they're interchangeable in that if you can't take pleasure in one, you probably can't take pleasure in the other.

BENNETT: So what food writers do you like?

BOURDAIN: [*Pauses*] Um . . .

BENNETT: Do you like Jeffrey Steingarten at all?

BOURDAIN: Yeah, now there's a guy, the authoritative crank done well. Really, really well. I kind of like Ruth Reichel's stuff. Not my style, but she makes it interesting because she's so kooky and writes about her own dysfunctional life. I also like the Nigella Lawson stuff. It's all about eating, she doesn't set herself up as an expert.

BENNETT: Do you like any of the classics, like M. F. K. Fisher?

BOURDAIN: Great writer. I've been accused of being more interested in chefs and in the lifestyle, than in the food, and that's true. Ludwig Bemelmans, George Orwell, Nicolas

Freling, they all write about chefs, and about the life. But, you know, if you're in the life, chances are you love food. I guess I'm more interested in the tribe of cooks, and their customs, attitudes, and argot, than I am in . . . well, you know, when you write about food it's like writing pornography. I mean, how many adjectives can you use to describe a salad? After "crunchy," "garden fresh," and "redolent of unkilled fields," what are you gonna do? It's like writing for Penthouse Letters.

BENNETT: One of your other apparent passions in fiction is writing about the mob. Does writing about the Mafia offer you a way to explore the characters, or do you think it's just fun to write and read about?

BOURDAIN: All of the above. I worked with a bunch of those guys back in the seventies and eighties. I'm a crime buff. I watch a lot of trials, I listen to wiretap recordings, read transcripts of surreptitious recordings of mobsters. First of all, I like the sound. To me, it's poetry, the sound of mobsters talking—especially when they think they might be being taped, but they're not sure, and they're speaking in that loopy, elliptical way. To me, Joe Pesci is like Charlie Parker: beautiful to listen to. So that's number one. Two, it's a pressure-cooker situation, with moral gray areas, personal loyalties . . . it's a more extreme version of life. What is the great American family television show? It's *The Sopranos*. There's no more accurate representation of the *average* American family. You have to go to an organized crime family to see what Americans really live like and how they talk at home. So, in a sense, it's just a comfortable way to explore the kind of social relationships I'm familiar with. Organized crime, much like real life, is not *The Godfather*. Somebody makes a mistake, they screw up, they don't get whacked, it's not the end of the world. People betray each other in small ways all the time. You make a decision, and you move on, you try to do the best you can. So it's a comfortable world, it's a familiar world, and it sounds good to me. I like the way they talk. They're funny guys. Almost all of them. And they eat, and eat well.

BENNETT: Although you do make fun of the way the mobsters eat in *Bone in the Throat*.

BOURDAIN: That was very much based on this kid I knew, a chef. There was a lot of me, a lot of chefs I worked with, but I was very much thinking of this hood-y character from Arthur Avenue who had become a French chef in New York. I thought it was very interesting that he was half in and half out. I was a kid who grew up with pirates and cowboys. The gangsters are simply a continuation of that tradition of *A Boy's Own Adventure*.

BENNETT: I like the conversational tone of both your fiction and non-fiction, and I've read in other interviews that you feel you developed your capacity for bullshitting in the restaurant world, in the kitchen. When you write, are you taking things from your own life and then "bullshitting" them out?

BOURDAIN: You're never going to find me writing about Irish potato farmers. I avoid any characters whose voices I can't do.

If I don't know them and how they talk, I'm not doing them. On the one hand, it's limiting, on the other, no, I don't see it as limiting. I've been in the business twenty-eight years, I've met a lot of people, I know how they talk. It's comfortable for me. Catchy, realistic dialogue is intensely important to me. More important than anything else. To hell with plot. If I'm reading a crime book for instance, like the Spenser books, and Spenser and the girlfriend start engaging in quippy repartee, catching up on the plot, it stops dead for me. Who talks like this in their private moments, in perfect sentences? I hate that. And also, when I'm imagining the reader, I'm always gearing it towards the kind of people who are like my characters. I'm writing for cooks, because I don't know who anyone else is. I haven't had that much exposure to the general public, I don't really know what they want, I wouldn't even know how to begin to try and please them. What I don't want is a salad man in some restaurant to read one of my books and say, "This is shit. Who talks like that?" If no one else, at least *I* talk like that.

BENNETT: So what mystery novelists do you like?

BOURDAIN: Crumley is great at his best. Daniel Woodrell. George Higgins. I think *The Friends of Eddie Coyle* is the absolute benchmark of pitch-perfect dialogue and atmosphere. You can smell the beer on these characters. I like my characters. I want to hang out with them. And I guess that's what I'm doing when I write fiction, is I'm creating a little world that I can escape into for a while, a more dramatic version of the world I've lived in. I can disappear in to their problems and move them around as I like. For me, George V. Higgins is the benchmark of absolutely perfect, unreliable dialogue. Everybody's kinda bullshitting. He owns that territory.

BENNETT: Do you like Ian Rankin?

BOURDAIN: He's a good friend. Perfect example of a guy who owns his territory. Don't be writing any crime books set in Edinburgh, because Rankin owns it. Higgins owns Boston, as far as I'm concerned. Woodrell owns the Ozarks. Rankin's got Edinburgh. Ellroy, at least in the past, he owned '40s-'50s L.A. I don't know *what* he owns now. I like that. Nobody's ever going to accuse those guys of getting the voice and the characters and the clothes wrong.

BENNETT: How much "bullshitting" creeps into your non-fiction?

BOURDAIN: I think when you use hyperbole as much as I do, a constant mea culpa is required. I think the most boring thing about my life is that I was a junkie. We've all read that book, that's why I didn't talk about it much. But I thought it was necessary in *Kitchen Confidential* to mention it: If I'm going to say all of these obnoxious, sweeping, bold statements about "the business" and the people in it, people should be reminded that, hey, this is a utility level ex-junkie talking to you here. So every word is true. Not that I'm not wrong about stuff. But as far as my own life, what I've seen, what people have said, for better or worse, it's all true.

BENNETT: It seems like the mafia world and the restaurant business as you write about them are these very male-dominated places where women can become tough and make it, but you don't see many "typical" women.

BOURDAIN: I guess they don't interest me. Some of the greatest moments in my professional career are when I've had the privilege of working with women who identified, absolutely correctly, the kitchen as a meritocracy, and said, "OK, boys, I'll play by these rules." And they kicked everybody's ass, as well they should and could. I greatly admire them. So, yeah, there is an archetypal woman in a lot of my books and she's largely constructed from pieces of my wife and women that I've worked with in the kitchen. I'm always a little dismayed when I go into a kitchen and it's a boys club except for the pastry section. It breaks my heart, because I want to see—not that it's my place to want or not want—but I would like to see women sauciers and women sous-chefs, women bossing around a bunch of Neanderthals who got an education real quick.

BENNETT: You must have an incredibly busy life, with book tours, TV—

BOURDAIN: Just filming the show is, like, six months out of my year.

BENNETT: When do you find time to write?

BOURDAIN: In the morning. And I take three months off in the Caribbean every year, or I try to. So I'll be taking notes or a diary or whatever while I'm on the road or whatever I'm working on, then I'll take two solid months in the Caribbean where I do nothing but pad around barefooted, wake up first thing in the morning and write for a few hours. You know, it's a carrot and stick. I can't leave the house, have a beer, or go to the beach until I put in the writing. The first three books I wrote, the reason I could write them is because I had no time to write them. I was working seventeen hours a day. I woke up, I started writing, got through as much as I could, then went to work. I didn't have any time to think about all those metaphysical aspects of writing: is it good, is it worthwhile, is it important—I didn't have time. Just wake up, do the job.

BENNETT: But why did you do that job?

BOURDAIN: Because I had the opportunity. I've never toiled away in a garret writing unpublished manuscripts. Absolutely everything I've ever written has been published. In almost every case, it started with either a short writing sample, a lucky break, or I wrote something short to entertain a limited audience, and an opportunity opened up where I could tell a story for money. Or love. And I could. I'm a hustler. I make the most of opportunities. Give me a crack at the bigs and I'll do my best.

BENNETT: In that sense, do you feel that the way you got into writing was similar to the way you came to be a chef?

BOURDAIN: I have exactly the same work ethic. I don't see writing as anything more important than cooking. In fact, I'm a little queasier on the writing. There's an element of shame, because it's so easy. I can't believe that people give me money for this shit. The TV, too. It's not work. At the end of the day, the TV show is the best job in the world. I get to go anywhere I want, eat and drink whatever I want. As long as I just babble at the camera, other people will pay for it. It's a gift. A few months ago, I was sitting cross-legged in the mountains of Vietnam with a bunch of Thai tribesman as a guest of honor drinking rice whiskey. Three years ago I never, ever in a million years thought that I would ever live to see any of that. So I know that I'm a lucky man.

MEDIUM RAW: IN CONVERSATION WITH ANTHONY BOURDAIN

INTERVIEW WITH JILL DUPLIEX
ON STAGE AT THE SYDNEY WRITERS' FESTIVAL
MAY 21, 2011

JILL DUPLIEX: I was looking to give a very quick introduction to Anthony for you, and I've found the most ideal one, online, existing on the Urban Dictionary, and I quote:

> "Anthony Bourdain (n) (adj); Anthony Bourdain is an author, chef, and television host. This is ironic because he is also Satan. He is one of the baddest motherfuckers to grace television. His books are well written, conscious, and can be quite humorous. His restaurant Les Halles serves amazing French Cuisine and is located in New York."

Ladies and gentlemen, Anthony Bourdain.

BOURDAIN: Thank you.

DUPLIEX: I'm not sure who's going to have as much, much fun up here. I think it's going to be me. Okay. You wrote your first book *Kitchen Confidential* in the year 2000 and it hit the *New York Times* Bestsellers List and you followed that with

A Cook's Tour, with *The Nasty Bits*, with crime novels, with TV shows. And now, this latest book *Medium Raw* is a sequel in effect to *Kitchen Confidential* 10 years on, part exposé, a memoir trekking life since leaving the kitchen. How have you changed in that last 10 years?

BOURDAIN: Well, when I wrote *Kitchen Confidential* I was a completely broke, stressed-out, forty-four-year-old working as he had always worked his entire life—in a not particularly great or famous restaurant kitchen, you know, standing next to a deep fryer . . . I'd never had health insurance, I'd never owned a car, I never paid my rent on time, I hadn't filed my taxes in ten years. I was a frightened, angry, desperate character who had seen almost nothing of the world outside of kitchens.

You know, it's ten years later, eleven years later, I've had almost ten years of the best job in the world, traveling around. I go anywhere I want, I've stayed in a lot of nice hotels, I've eaten in some of the best restaurants in the world, I'm friends with a lot of the greatest chefs, I've seen life high and low . . . I've lived a life of incredible—almost overnight from who I was back then, my life changed so drastically! You know I'm older, I don't know that I'm wiser, but I've seen a hell of a lot more than I ever thought I would have seen. I've become corrupted by the process in the sense that I've become one of those TV characters that I had no understanding of at all when I was in the kitchen. And maybe the largest difference, you know, I'm a daddy now! I have a four-year-old little girl at home. You know, all the clichés about parenthood are of course absolutely true.

DUPLIEX: So one of the big changes is of course that you were a chef and now you're a celebrity . . .

BOURDAIN: I don't work for a living. I mean . . .

DUPLIEX: You're making it sound good.

BOURDAIN: I mean, writing—I have no sympathy for anyone fortunate enough to get paid *any kind of money* to write whining about writer's block or how hard it is, or some sort of internal torture. You're doing it in a sitting position, so right away, you know? I spent my whole adult life on my feet. I feel very, very lucky that anybody even gives a shit what I think. It's not something I'm used to, and it is a privilege to be able to write and have even eight people care what you're saying.

DUPLIEX: There's a great line in *Medium Raw* where you said being a heroin addict was fantastic preparation for being a celebrity.

BOURDAIN: Yeah!

DUPLIEX: [*Laughing*] Could you please explain?

BOURDAIN: Well, particularly in the world of television, but it's also true I think in any media: there are a lot of people out there who are full of shit. People will tell you, *especially* in Hollywood, you know, they're telling me, "We love your work," "We really want to work with you," "We're terribly excited about this new project"—all of those things. You know, when you're a junkie it is necessary that you very quickly—because you're desperate, you only have ten dollars and you need to get well with it and you're buying it on the street from some pretty hardcore characters, you're surrounded by hustlers with a real imperative to hustle—you just develop a sort of a sixth sense. You become a pretty good judge of character: Is this person reliable, or are they full of shit? Are they the sort of person who is going to do what they say they're going to do? And you develop this sort of feral sense, which I think is true of chefs as well. You look into someone's eyes and you ask yourself—you believe there are only two kinds of people in this world. There are the type of people who say they're going to do something tomorrow and they actually do it, and then there's everybody else. And having been a heroin addict you have to develop at least some skills as far as judging which type of person that it might be you're dealing with, or you end up dead, or well, you don't end up on the street very long.

DUPLIEX: Do you think that's why you were drawn to the kitchen or to the restaurant industry in the first place? To get some sort of structure?

BOURDAIN: I fell into the business accidentally. But it was certainly the only time in my life that I responded well to any kind of structure. I was grateful for it. It was the first time that I went home with any reason to be proud of myself. It was the first time that I cared about anybody else's opinion of me. It was the first time I respected myself or anybody else. It was definitely the perfect mix of romance and, you know, piratical attitudes, and sex, and drugs, and rock and roll—that's true. But you're absolutely right. It was that structure, it was that first hierarchy and structure, and quantifiable organization, and value system, that I recognized that I needed it, and I was grateful for it. And I liked it, obviously. I fell in love with the life long before I started to get serious about food.

DUPLIEX: But it's that anger, isn't it, that you brought to your writing in a way? And that's what made the writing so compelling, because it was very short, very direct, very short order in a way, very direct, very no-bullshit about your life. You had a lot of—

BOURDAIN: A lot of hyperbole. You know, in the kitchen, as a chef, when you're angry at a cook or a waiter, they are for the moment, the worst, most miserable rat bastard on earth. But five minutes later, I love you, I want to bear your children, you are the greatest human being who ever walked the Earth. Those feelings can coexist or change pretty quickly. But you know I *am* angry. Clearly that fuels me. But I like to think that—like a number of other authors I can think of—the flip side of that is a sense of spoiled Romanticism, a disappointment with the way the world turned out. You know, it was supposed to be far more beautiful and romantic, and gentle, and I learned pretty early on it wasn't going to be like that.

DUPLIEX: And now you punish people.

BOURDAIN: Yeah! Well, you know, it doesn't make everything better to insult somebody, but . . . it helps.

[*Audience laughter*]

DUPLIEX: I'm going to throw you another question about this whole celebrity chef caper, because it is so much a part of our world at the moment. We had Marco Pierre White in town this week, you've described him as an icon, an iconic figure in our gastronomic universe. And yet here he was in Australia flogging Continental Stock Cubes, which broke my heart because I fell in love with him at the beginning—he was the hottest young chef I'd ever seen in my life and his food was just so beautiful and his head was in a very great place. But he's a fucked up character, too. But—

BOURDAIN: Well, we all are, anyone who cooks.

DUPLIEX: Yes, we are, we are. But I found that a bit depressing. I mean he's probably thinking he's doing good business, and he's running around the world and doing all that. But do you think that that is the trajectory of someone who—

BOURDAIN: Why should we hold chefs—Cooking is *hard*. It's really hard. It breaks you down. A chef's lifespan used to be, in the thirties, was thirty-seven years old. It is now about fifty-seven. Why do we demand, or insist, or expect chefs to die behind the stove, broken-assed, flat-footed, varicose veined, at fifty-seven? Why do we hold chefs to a higher standard than Keith Richards, or Iggy, or anyone else who's incredibly cool and changed the world?

You know, Marco Pierre White—I would compare him to Orson Welles. Orson Welles made *Citizen Kane*. If he wants to end up making commercials for bad wine, good for him. I wish he'd been paid more money for it. He still made the greatest goddamn movie in American history to that point. He changed the world for the better. Marco has done his good works. What I admire about Marco in particular is that he reached the mountaintop—he got three stars* earlier than I think just about anyone else in the world had ever done. An Englishman who had never been to France cooking French food—and he didn't want it anymore. He gave his stars back and said I've done my thing. I was to spend my days cashing checks, walking around in the English country-side shooting animals.

[*Audience laughter*]

DUPLIEX: That's true.

BOURDAIN: And you know what? God bless him. Who better deserves to sell out any way they want, make a little money in their old age, than chefs?

DUPLIEX: Okay, but—

[*Applause*]

BOURDAIN: I mean, I'll say this: I feel a lot better about Marco Pierre White cashing paychecks now for whatever he may do than for Paris Hilton getting paid for *anything*.

---

* Michelin stars, a rating system used by France's Michelin Guides series. Three stars is the highest rating, and rarely granted.

[*Applause*]

DUPLIEX: It's true. Yeah, absolutely. However, where do you draw the line? Do you have a personal line in the sand that you will not cross, or is there some level of behavior that you go, "That chef can do this, can do that, can flog bad wine," et cetera—is there a line where you go—

BOURDAIN: Okay, we all have a—let's make it personal. There is a line for me: You know, Olive Garden, or Kentucky Fried Chicken . . . I would have a very hard time personally standing there saying this food is really delicious when I know it's crap.

DUPLIEX: So, lying.

BOURDAIN: No, I'm happy to lie. [*Audience laughter*] It is not an integrity issue with me. It is a vanity issue. I don't care how much money in the world, I've had plenty—I know what it's like to wake up in the morning ashamed of what I did yesterday and I don't like that feeling. It's just, I don't want to look in the mirror and see the Olive Garden or the TGI Friday guy. I just, it's vanity. It doesn't have anything to do with integrity.

DUPLIEX: Okay. My line for that, my line if they cross then I lose sight of them, the point of no return, is going on *Dancing With the Stars*.

BOURDAIN: Ah! Well I've been offered twice.

DUPLIEX: Offered twice?

BOURDAIN: Twice.

DUPLIEX: Again, it's probably a vanity issue . . . ?

BOURDAIN: Yeah, I mean, I'm not going on *Celebrity Rehab* yet, either. [*Audience laughter*] But, you know, talk to me in ten years. I mean, I'm doing well now!

DUPLIEX: Yep, it's true. And I will. Okay, as a chef, what's your idea of the customer from hell?

BOURDAIN: The customer from hell, the worst customer on earth, is the customer who's decided beforehand, they're already miserable the minute they walk in the door. And they've decided that they're gonna feel better if they bully, speak condescendingly to, or mistreat floor staff. This is an unforgivable act to me. I mean if we go out to lunch together and you're rude to your waiter and treat them like a piece of shit, talk down to them, or blame them for the kitchen's mistakes, our relationship is dead and will always be dead. That sort of person working through personal issues—they're not there to relax, get a little drunk and let things happen, have a meal. They're just a miserable person who will probably bring that same misery to ruin every experience whether it's a musical performance, or the food, a dinner, or the sex act.

[*Audience laughter*]

DUPLIEX: Quite. And do you have an idea of a chef from hell?

BOURDAIN: The chef from hell is the chef who's been broken and just doesn't care, you know? They have no pride, they're unhappy, they don't like their customers, they don't like their owner, they don't care whether their customers are happy anymore—I've been there! You know, all pride is gone . . . A heartbroken chef is the chef from hell.

Because almost all of them start out wanting to make good food, and for many, many years you were punished for that. You know, if you dared to try to serve food the way you knew it to be great, that you'd had it in France, or the way your training had taught you, you'd get slapped down by the customer. You know: There's still blood in this steak! Tuna? That's for cats! Squid? Ew, it's ookie! Fish is oily and dark! You know, these were very much the common attitudes back in the 70s and 80s, so I think a good side effect of this admittedly annoying celebrity chef phenomenon is that people actually give a shit about what the chef thinks now, and are willing to give them a shot. But the one who's out there toiling, just kind of slopping it out and doesn't really care . . . that's the chef from hell.

DUPLIEX: And is there such a thing as a novelist or a writer from hell for you?

BOURDAIN: Um . . . I don't know. I don't really know many writers. I don't hang out with writers. I mean, ask yourself, you're in a lifeboat adrift in the sea about to wash up on an island—which would you prefer to be marooned on an island with, a bunch of cooks or a bunch of writers?

[Audience laughter]

You know I enjoy a good book as much as, if not *more than*, anybody . . . but writers? [*laughing*] I have mixed emotions.

DUPLIEX: Okay, well, related to that I guess: restaurant critics. You've said a few mean things about restaurant critics in your day.

BOURDAIN: Well, in general it is a degraded profession. I've known a lot of bent—you know you said in the dressing room there are venal sins versus . . .

DUPLIEX: [*Addressing the audience*] Well, Anthony got into a bit of trouble for calling restaurant critics corrupt, and I actually said I've never met any restaurant critics that are venally—financially—corrupt, but I have met some that are what I'd call socially corrupt. So that they *do* have relationships with chefs, restaurateurs—

BOURDAIN: So, there's a difference. First of all, there are plenty of food writers I know—*The New York Times* critic—that year after year after year, they go to extraordinary measures to insulate themselves from the swamp. Certainly, Jonathan Gold* is a hero of mine . . . I can think of a lot of people off-hand who I would exclude from that description. But there are those who, I mean I know food critics also who demand free vacations, for instance—"I would like a free vacation in

---

* Jonathan Gold (1960-2018) was a food and restaurant critic for *Gourmet* magazine and the *Los Angeles Times*

the Caribbean for my wife and myself"—demanding from the subjects of their reviews. Imagine! "You know, I'd really like a five-day vacation. I understand you're working with a hotel in the Caribbean. You know my wife and I would really enjoy a week down there all expenses paid, with bungalow, and free room service . . . Can you arrange that?"

DUPLIEX: Are you talking about anyone in particular?

BOURDAIN: Mmm, that's hypothetical speaking. [*Audience laughter*] Your libel laws here—I think it's libel tourism, right? You could sue if you get bad reviews, so I'm gonna leave that alone. There are people who, back in the day, and some of these characters are still around, who I can well remember shaking restaurateurs down for cash. But much more common are the people who become corrupted by what is inevitably a corrupting process. It would be impossible for me to be a food critic, okay? All my friends are chefs. I've been compromised by my personal relationships with these chefs over the years. My palate has become corrupted, because unlike most of you I've eaten at El Bulli* a lot. I've eaten at Robuchon†. To me, a 12-course tasting menu at one of the great restaurants in the world is often a burden. I'm bored with truffles.

[*Audience laughter*]

---

* El Bulli was an award-winning restaurant located in the Catalonian countryside. It was known for its association with molecular gastronomy, and was run by several well-known chefs, perhaps most notably Ferran Adrià. It closed in 2011.

† Jöel Robuchon (1945-2018) was a French chef and restauranteur who operated restaurants around the world. He won more Michelin stars (32) than any other chef.

What kind of critical ability can I, what can I say that is meaningful to an ordinary person when I've lost my ability to be delighted by things that to most others would be a once-in-a-lifetime and incredible experience? But the most common form of corruption is of course just like reporters, you know, White House correspondents—the pressure is on food writers. I don't want to write about my favorite lemon meringue pie every week. I don't want to write muffin recipes. I want to go to restaurants and live a good life and write interesting things. In order to do that I need access. I need people in that life to tell me things. Now these people have their own interests which is, I want food critics to write good things about me. So I'm going to send you a few extra snacks, I'm going to take you for a little private tour of my kitchen, we'll have special little candlelight meals together where I'll preview my new menu, maybe I'm gonna give you a backrub, invite you over to my house . . .

[*Audience laughter*]

You know, at the end of the day you're going to be less likely to say anything bad about me. There's a popular food guide in New York, it's the industry standard. Every high-end restaurant in New York buys them by the thousands—five, six thousand copies of this guide. And if they don't buy five or six this year, they get a call saying, "How come you're not buying as many?" "Well, you weren't so nice to me this year." "That's okay, we'll fix it." . . . That ain't right, you know? So, when a journalist needs access and the only access they're going to get is, especially when they're not getting paid to eat at these restaurants a lot—they don't have as much of a budget as, say, the *Times,* do to go out to fine dining restaurants—they rely on their subjects to give them good stuff. Whether that's money, or free food, or extra courses, but more often than not just access. And if they don't get it, some of them tend to get cranky. And then there's payback involved. So, I don't think it's necessarily the most evil thing in the world, but I think it's useful if you're writing about food, certainly if you're critiquing food, maybe there should be term limits.

DUPLIEX: Term limits?

BOURDAIN: Yeah, maybe after five years you should gracefully move on to some other sector. Because you've been swimming in the same sort of blood temperature hot tub for a long time—you're gonna catch something.

[*Audience laughter*]

DUPLIEX: Well I suppose the restaurant critic is in some sort of position between the restaurant industry, the chef, the kitchen, and us the diners, and it's just trying to explain one to the other a little bit in many ways. And that is your unique position, as well, because as a chef you know what's going on out there, and yet as a writer you're at the front many times observing quite rigorously what's going on.

There's one story in *Medium Raw*, my favorite, that is simply a morning in the life of a fish filleter in a restaurant in New York called Le Bernardin. The fish comes in in the morning, this guy's got his knives, he fillets the fish, he places it in the way the chefs want it, ready to go for their lunch—that's it. That's the entire story. But actually, had a chef written it, with all the knowledge of what had to go down, it could still be boring. If a writer, a journalist, a rigorous observer, had written it, it could still be boring. But somebody who can fuse those two things with respect—so much respect was coming off the pages about this guy because he's so good at what he does—

BOURDAIN: A thousand pounds of fish this guy cleans in four hours, every day—

DUPLIEX: Yes! It's a beautiful story.

BOURDAIN:—off the bone, and into perfect, three-star Michelin portions. It takes three trained sous chefs all day long, seven hours—three of 'em working together—to replace this guy when he goes on vacation. But this is a perfect example! I would have never been able to write that, I never would have had access to this guy, I never would have known about him if I hadn't been best friends with Eric Ripert,* and been in this weird, compromised—the very thing that allowed me to write that was the fact that I should never be trusted to be a critic of a restaurant. . . I live in a half world, you know?

DUPLIEX: Yeah, yeah, between heaven and hell there's a chaos . . .

---

* Eric Ripert is a French chef known for his abilities as poissonier, and as the head chef and proprietor of Le Bernardin in New York City, a three-star Michelin restaurant that is regularly noted on best-of lists in culinary magazines as one of the world's top restaurants, and as the "Temple of Seafood."

BOURDAIN: Life is good. I like my job.

DUPLIEX: I like the Urban Dictionary because they went on to say "on his TV shows, he's known for eating way too much yet being tall and skinny, smoking excessively," so this was written a few years ago, "and getting drunk most everywhere he goes. [*Bourdain laughs*] He can also be extremely obnoxious and arrogant when doing any of these three things." But you're not, are you?

BOURDAIN: I can be, I—

DUPLIEX: He's been so well mannered, we're all so disappointed.

[*Audience laughter*]

BOURDAIN: Umm, I can be, I can be really obnoxious—

DUPLIEX: But you're not exactly biting the heads off chooks* or screwing the waitress over the hot grill.

BOURDAIN: You know, that's so last week? [*Bourdain laughs*] I mean, I'm older now, you know? First of all, I'm the father of a little girl. That means a lot to me. I'm not gonna apologize for my previous life—that's what daddy was, that's what daddy did—but I don't want her reading terrible shit about

---

* Chickens.

me on the internet, behaving badly towards women, for instance. I'm not gonna do that.

You know, I was referred to, when *Kitchen Confidential* came out, as a "bad boy chef." Now, I was *forty-four years old* when that book came out, so already it was ludicrous. I never really took it that seriously. And I'm certainly not that bad, I'm certainly not a boy, and I'm not even a chef anymore! But one of the reasons I wrote this book was to kind of correct that impression. But I think I've benefited very much from the fact that *Kitchen Confidential* was so over-testosterone and so obnoxious. I didn't think anyone would read it outside of the restaurant business so it was written for the consumption and entertainment of my fry cook, essentially—that was the only person I could ever imagine buying a copy. So it was intended to be entertaining and amusing to a very tiny group of people who were working in New York restaurants, and the tone reflected that. It would sound softer and more familiar to them.

But I benefited from—because the book was so obnoxious, people are surprised when I can eat with a knife and fork and not bark obscenities indiscriminately at least. You know I benefit very much from low expectations.

[Audience laughter]

DUPLIEX: The voice in all the books is very strong. Were you born with that voice? Is that your natural voice? Do you write as you speak, speak as you write or did you have early influences, did you have something to model yourself on?

BOURDAIN: I'm gonna tell you something that aspiring writers or writers here will really hate me for: I've never written anything in my life that hasn't been published.

DUPLIEX: Yeah, we hate you.

BOURDAIN: I have never toiled away in a garret for years writing unsuccessful or unpublished manuscripts. I wrote the article that *Kitchen Confidential* was based on for a free paper in New York. I figured they were lame enough to buy my piece. It ended up in the *New Yorker*. I got lucky. I'm always talking, telling stories. Being a little provocateur with a way with words was something that was true of me when I was a little kid. I've always used that skill to get the things I want, to manipulate events to my liking, to get myself into trouble, to get myself out of trouble, to hurt my enemies, to seduce people, or make people do things I would like them to do. So I was always a little . . . you know, my parents very early on said "You should really be a lawyer, you've got such a way with words."

I write like I talk. But yeah I pretty much . . . Yeah, I've always been like this.

DUPLIEX: Right.

BOURDAIN: If there were influences, writing influences, who really turned on the light for me—I always did read a lot—certainly you can hear Hunter Thompson in my writing. When I was twelve years old I opened *Rolling Stone* magazine where they were serializing what then became *Fear and Loathing in Las Vegas*, and that clicked for me. His rage, that someone could write, could put into words the way I felt—this *bitter* disappointment with the way the sixties turned out. The hyperbole, the lush, violent language, the humor—clearly that was an influence. But he was maybe not the best role model for a twelve year old. [*Audience laughter*] I sought to emulate him in all ways but actually writing, you know. I just figured maybe if I take a lot of drugs for the next thirty years, I'll be able to write like that! [*Bourdain laughs*]

But he was also a cautionary tale because I think I learned that—by the time the book hit—I realized I don't want to end up like Hunter Thompson either. I'm not gonna go out there and play the bad boy chef, you know, and get paid for it. I'm just, you know . . . You'll notice the most perverse thing I've been able to do the last few years, I'm very proud of is, I've done a couple of really fuzzy, warm, family-friendly shows. I say that'll really stick it to my fans. They'll be so disappointed.

[*Audience laughter*]

DUPLIEX: Yep. You've also eaten some very strange things in your life and I don't want to say "Okay, what's the worst thing you've ever eaten?" So, instead, I'm going to give you a list of some of the nastiest things—

BOURDAIN: Quick fire? Love that.

DUPLIEX: —in the world, okay, and you just tell me if you've had them and if it's relevant, what they tasted like. Because you might have swallowed some, you might have spit, I don't know. Okay! Sheep testicles.

BOURDAIN: Had 'em, delicious, good texture, much better than beef nuts.

[*Audience laughter*]

DUPLIEX: Good to know. Seal eyeballs.

BOURDAIN: Good when fresh, like good quality sushi. In context, it could be a heartwarming family experience.

[*Audience laughter*]

DUPLIEX: The beating heart of a giant cobra.

BOURDAIN: I've said it's like an angry, over-athletic oyster. Is it food, or is it some sort of weird boner medicine for anxious Asians? I kind of regret it.

DUPLIEX: You regret that?

BOURDAIN: Not much going on there flavor wise. You know, what are your expectations? [*laughing*] It's more like a weird male bonding, is-it-medicine or is-it-food kind of situation. I wouldn't do it again. It wasn't bad, it wasn't an unpleasant experience, but you know . . . poor cobra.

DUPLIEX: Yeah, yep . . . Um, the unwashed rectum or anus of a warthog.

BOURDAIN: Okay. It tasted exactly like you would expect it to taste.

[*Audience laughter*]

DUPLIEX: Yeah, that's what I was afraid of.

BOURDAIN: But this was a—I knew I was going to be ill, I did get very ill, I knew it was going to be terrible, but this was a tribal situation. I'm a good guest.

DUPLIEX: You are, you're very well mannered.

BOURDAIN: I'm in a tribal situation, the whole tribe was looking at me, the chief is handing me the best, most treasured part, it's taken him three days to track this thing—I'm taking one for the team.

DUPLIEX: [*Laughing*] Oh yeah.

BOURDAIN: I'm actually polite in such circumstances.

DUPLIEX: Yes.

BOURDAIN: You know, I do something called the "grandma rule"—if I'm at grandma's house I will eat what grandma offers and I will say yes grandma it's delicious I'll have seconds. I passed on the seconds this time [*laughing*] but I did my best to soldier through.

DUPLIEX: That was in . . .

BOURDAIN: Namimbia. In the Kalahari with the bushmen.

DUPLIEX: In Iceland there's a thing called a stinking rotten fermented shark . . .

BOURDAIN: Rotten, rotten shark

DUPLIEX: . . . that you can smell from ten kilometers.

BOURDAIN: Yeah. It's unspeakably vile. Gill and I were both—A. A. Gill and I were both asked the other day[*] what's the worst the worst thing you've ever tasted. We both agreed. That is just far and away, it's just, it's that reek of ammonia and urine, it's beyond—they handle it with gloves! I mean, they don't even touch the stuff when they serve it to you!

DUPLIEX: But that's mostly the smell surely?

BOURDAIN: No, it's the flavor. Unlike durian[†], for instance, that smells like hell but to my mind tastes awesome, has something real going for it, something wonderful—this tastes just as bad as it smells. And I don't think anyone actually likes it. It's a nod to their proud, Viking roots and harder, more austere times when this was the only way they could preserve protein during the summer months. I mean, you

---

[*] Bourdain had done a speaking event with Adrian Anthony Gill, the noted British food writer, two days earlier at the Festival.

[†] Durian is a notoriously foul-smelling fruit found in southeast Asia.

see them handling it with gloves, they put it in their mouth, and they chase it with this big shot of, like, rocket fuel—you know, how good can it be?

DUPLIEX: Well you would, yeah . . . All right, well now I do have to ask you what's the worst thing apart from all those? Because I have heard you give a different answer . . .

BOURDAIN: Well I mean, would I eat rotten shark before I ate a Chicken McNugget? Um . . . I'd feel better about myself eating the rotten shark.

DUPLIEX: Yes, you would.

BOURDAIN: You know, I feel compromised, a part of an evil empire, when I eat a McNugget. There's something morally wrong about it. And it's just—what is it? What part of the chicken does it come from?

[*Audience laughter*]

DUPLIEX: All those other things we talked about you knew exactly what they were and where, particularly where, they had come from. And so the thing that scares you the most is the . . .

BOURDAIN: I'm scared that my daughter, the thought of my daughter eating one and liking it just fills me with terror. It is—we should feed our enemies Chicken McNuggets.

[*Audience laughter*]

You know, Osama Bin Laden wouldn't have lasted anywhere near this long if he just had, you know, a regular Mc-
Nugget diet. You know, Tora Bora, he wouldn't have been
able to squeeze his fat ass into a cave. [*Audience laughter*] We
would have seen him from space! [*Bourdain laughs*]

DUPLIEX: The drones would have seen him, yeah.

BOURDAIN: Yeah!

DUPLIEX: So you spend your life traveling around the world.
Now, do you feel an urgency at the moment to get out to certain countries relatively quickly before their street food, their
authentic regional food, all the things that you're going for to
try, while they're still around and before they start turning
into Chicken McNuggets?

BOURDAIN: I don't know, I'm kind of optimistic about the
future of the world. It's one of those things I—you know,
the Chinese are increasingly buying everything in America,
and buying all of our real estate and certainly all of our debt,
and a lot of people are frightened. Will they come over here,
and you know, pretty soon, they'll be all over the place!
Well, we'll be eating a lot better. A *lot* better. So I think the
expanding Asian influence, this power shift away from the
West to the East, is probably, to me, at least for food, argu-
ably a good thing!
     I mean Singapore may be Disneyland with the death

penalty, as I think R. W. Apple* called it, but it is a foodie wonderland. And they figured out—they are the nanniest of nanny states and they've got all of the same concerns you have here, about hygiene and zoning, and what if oh-my-god it might hurt you, we better make it illegal. You know, like the cheese situation here which is so shameful, or the oyster situation here which is so shameful. But they figured it out. You know, the food court in Singapore, to me, is a shining beacon of how we could live in a perfect world. So, I'm encouraged!

The places that I feel like I'm rushing to before they change, I mean, I'm not sentimental about Communism, I'm no big fan of the regime in Cuba, but I sure as hell wanted to see it before it changed. And it was indeed, it *is* indeed, something extraordinary. But the food scene there, you know—not so great. People are really, really hungry. I'd like to get to Burma then Myanmar but that's a situation where I'm waiting for the government to change. I'd like to get to Tehran as soon as possible, but again, not right now.

DUPLIEX: Yeah, exactly. So you're a bit like a canary, really, that we can send out into the world—

BOURDAIN: [*Laughs*] Yeah, when I keel over you'll all know: don't go there!

DUPLIEX: Yeah, exactly. Don't go there! But, okay, if you are that canary and you are one of the first to note, in our food

* An acclaimed *New York Times* reporter and editor who wrote about politics, travel, and food, and was a renowned gourmand.

world, various changes, or drops of temperature, or cultural sort of shifts—is there anything your nose is telling you at the moment?

BOURDAIN: Paris is fun again. You can eat really, really well in Paris. You know, fifteen years ago they were rude, particularly to Americans, and it would cost you forty euros for a bowl of soup at a really good restaurant. You know, just spectacularly expensive. Now you can eat a terrific, world-class, Michelin-quality meal for forty euros, thirty euros, fifty euros, and they'll even be nice to you—in a casual setting.

DUPLIEX: Yeah, we love a global financial crisis, don't we?

BOURDAIN: But it's these young chefs, you know—the gastronomy movement is really exciting. David Chang is a big influence in Paris. You hear French Chefs saying "Oh yes, we'd like this man David Chang, from New York." This was *unthinkable* fifteen years ago, that, you know, any French chef would even acknowledge that Spain existed much less New York! [*audience laughter*] So that's an exciting place to eat. Certainly, I see Singapore as a hopeful, culinarily, as a hopeful example, as an alternative. That's fast food, too. It's also *good food.*

Um, places I've been excited about . . . Tukey is amazing. I'd like to see more good Turkish food. You know, a wider range of Turkish foods than the usual suspects. Um . . . Brazil . . . Columbia—just in general, go to Columbia. It's awesome. I went to Medellin which, ten years ago, was the worst place on Earth. The murder capital of the world. And now it is really—I came out of Columbia really optimistic about the world. Wow, it's possible to improve a really fucked-up place in a short period of time. You know, there's no excuse for inner city Detroit, having been to Medellin.

DUPLIEX: I think the beautiful girl on *Modern Family*'s done an awful lot for Colombian tourism as well. [*Bourdain laughs*] But, tell me, I mean, they're famous, they export all their coffee beans to here, amongst other places—did you get a decent coffee in Columbia?

BOURDAIN: Yeah, but it was the food and the people. I mean, these are inseparable. Listen, I love food, I'm guilty of being a food pornographer, I fetishize it—but it is only one part of a full life.

You know, recently I married into a large, Italian, Sardinian family, and seeing how they live, their relationship with alcohol, and with food, and ingredients, has really been an education, you know? Good food, at whatever income level, is a birthright to them. Gotta have it. Wine with every meal, must have. But you never see drunk-ass Italians staggering around vomiting in the streets. They do everything in proportion. They understand that it's about good food and good liquor, but also hopefully you're getting laid on a regular basis and you're having good conversation and there's music somewhere, and company, and you know . . . those are all part of a thing. A life.

DUPLIEX: The reason you like Paris at the moment is, as you said, that next generation of chefs. Are you picking up that this generational change is actually changing *all* the cities around the world and *all* the different food cultures, restaurant cultures.

BOURDAIN: Well look how differently, you know, look how different the kinds of businesses that are popping up here now—you know, a lot of these people who are opening up small places, or pop ups or just little, you know, stripped-to-the-bone casual eateries, they're cooking their hearts out with maybe one other cook or a dishwasher. Listen, in the end of course they'll give in, they'll open a 300-seat restaurant, and they *will* have a place in a casino, and they *will* have a cookbook and a boil-in-a-bag dinner line. You know, Robuchon, and all the great French—Roger Vergé*—all of those people started out that way, too. But what we're getting is a lot more of 'em and, you know, it's just good times. It's part of cyclical wave, and we're eating—it's certainly new to *us*, in the English-speaking world. So, you know, to my way of thinking there's never been a better time to cook in the English-speaking world and there's certainly never been a better time to eat.

DUPLIEX: Adrian Gill was talking the other day about that most depressing term, "fine dining"—you know, the chef likes to serve this warm, etc.—and he said, in this voice of wonderment, "And we let them get away with it!" Which I thought was gorgeous. So—chef hat back on—what do you think of this current restaurant trend towards fusing art and landscape and technology on the plate?

---

* Roger Vergé (1930–2015) was one of the most influential chefs and restauranteurs of the 20th century, renowned as one of the creators of nouvelle cuisine. At his restaurant Moulin de Mougins in the French Riviera, he trained numerous chefs that went on to fame, including David Bouley, Alain Ducasse, and David Boulud.

BOURDAIN: It depends, I mean—ask yourself before you start dabbling with what somebody somewhere is calling molecular gastronomy: Am I a genius? Am I Ferran Adrià?* Am I anywhere near as talented and as visionary and as firmly rooted in a place with as much food culture as Catalonia . . . or am I just kinda jerking off here?

[Audience laughter]

You know, I love Jimi Hendrix. Can I, will I, ever play guitar as well as Jimi Hendrix? Because you better. If you're gonna mess around with that stuff, my way of feeling is don't try. Find your own style.

A lot of those styles are going to end up standard practice in the industry, you know—sous vide for sure, a few others. I think people misunderstand Adrià for sure. But you know, short answer, some of the very worst, most painful meals of my life have been with people, talented young chefs, who become over-impressed and over-enthusiastic about a cargo cult version of what they believe to be happening at places like El Bulli and they're just playing out of their depth.

DUPLIEX: But there is surely an opportunity, surely, for those young chefs to adopt the technology but then turn it 'round and use where they are and who they are to create something new.

BOURDAIN: Yeah. I'll come back to Dave Chang, Wylie Dufresne, people like that who, you know, they cherry pick:

---

* The highly-regarded Spanish chef often associated with molecular gastronomy. He was, for many years, the head chef at the El Bulli restaurant in Catalonia.

"Hey, that looks really interesting! We can make a really delicious dish that's actually soulful and reminds people of their childhood, but we're using a technique that Ferran Adrià developed." Nothing, nothing wrong with that. It's when it becomes like an eye gouging experience, you know it's something hanging on the edge of a long prong and it's not very good. You know, if it takes your waiter ten minutes to describe the dish and two minutes to eat it . . .

[*Audience laughter*]

Is it fun? That's all. Is it fun and is it delicious? If the answer is yes then I'm for it.

DUPLIEX: You've recently written, not quite an episode, but scenes, a sort of a stream, for an amazing television series called *Treme*, which must be—Oh and your face lights up every time somebody says *Treme*!—it must be a thrill. I mean, it's a thrill to watch the bloody thing so it must be a thrill to write for it.

BOURDAIN: I found suddenly, I don't know when it happened, but I found myself at this weird point in my career where I realized that . . . opportunities would pop up to work with really amazing people who I really admire, or *worship*. And you know, I can actually, you know, just to hang out with some of these people is, is—you know, I'm stammering here. So out of the blue, I mean, to me, *The Wire* was the greatest thing ever in the history of television. I mean, there's never been a better use of the television medium, never been a better dramatic series. So to get a call out of the blue form David Simon was just this devastat—

DUPLIEX: That happened like that? He just rang out of the blue?

BOURDAIN: Yeah. "Would you be interested in doing some writing for me?" It was like you're a football fan, you're home, you're a little kid, you're a football fan and David Beckham calls up and says, you know, "Let's kick the ball around." You know, I teared up, I hyperventilated, I would have done it for free. And in fact, there are a few things that I'm doing in my life right now where, you know, it's not about the money. It's really . . . fun. It's the most fun I've ever had writing or doing any kind of work, working with people much smarter than me, these incredibly creative people, it's just . . . You know it's like you get invited to join the cool kids. And, um, so I am.

I'm doing a graphic novel with a really amazing artist named Langdon Foss and a friend of mine named Joel Rose, because, you know, it's not gonna make me rich, I'm doing it because I can, and it's fun and I like comics and, you know, it's cool.

DUPLIEX: And you've set up your own TV production company for your own TV—

BOURDAIN: I'm partners in a production company that I started with—the camera people on my first series of *A Cook's*

Tour and I all quit Food Network at the same time because we'd set up a show with Ferran Adrià and the network was not interested. So, they go like "Who is this guy? He talks funny, he's from Spain, it's too smart for us, we're not interested." So we all reached in our own pockets—we figured well we've set this up, we're gettin' this. This is history here, we have incredible, amazing, once-in-a-lifetime access, we're getting this show up. We had no customer, no money, we just reached in our own pockets and went out and shot a documentary about the experience. And that was the beginning of this entity that then that continues to create *No Reservations*, the same group of people.

So really, we owe it all to Ferran. If he hadn't said, "Yes, I invite you to come into my life and film it," I might be riding a pony from barbeque competitions to barbecue competitions on Food Network . . .

DUPLIEX: Bringing out a line of burgers or something, yeah, we look forward to that. The Bourdain Burger line.

BOURDAIN: [*Laughs*] Yeah, not gonna happen. Not in this life.

ANTHONY BOURDAIN DISHES ON FOOD

INTERVIEW WITH NEIL DEGRASSE TYSON
STARTALK WITH NEIL DEGRASSE TYSON
APRIL 7, 2013

NEIL DEGRASSE TYSON: People always say "Oh, I've been to this country, and this food is a delicacy there." That's a cue to me that the food tastes nasty, or it's some bug that they pulled out of the ground and sautéed. So, what's with people saying something is a delicacy?

ANTHONY BOURDAIN: Well, it's rare or expensive, you know? It's valued more than the way we look at shrimp or lobster or truffles as the good stuff, a lot of people in this world look at ingredients that many of us would probably have some difficulty with. That's an attitude that changes really quickly . . . the more you travel. You know, that's something I got over very quickly. Particularly, you know, you talk about, wow, their food in Thailand is really repulsive to me. I mean, they eat bugs! But the Thais, who are largely a non-dairy culture, you know, try to put yourself in their shoes. They're looking at us—you know, eating, like, cottage cheese or Roquefort would be truly horrifying, if you think about it for a second, what that must look like.

DEGRASSE TYSON: What I do find interesting though, is you go from one country to the next, and one of the simplest measures of this is what is the assortment of flavors they infuse in their potato chips that they're selling. So like in Japan, they have fish-flavored potato chips. I mean, we eat fish here, but I don't know that that would sell.

BOURDAIN: There are whole spectrums of flavors that other countries, other cultures, take for granted and require in their diet. In the Philippines there's a whole *bitter* component that we are almost instinctively not happy with. They will introduce bile into dishes to give it that welcome bitter note. There's a tradition of rotting things, like fermenting fish, getting it really, offensively funky by our standards, just 'cause, I think, out of boredom.

DEGRASSE TYSON: It introduces another flavor.

BOURDAIN: And it's worth noting also that we—Western societies, anyway—used to do that. For the Roman times, the condiment of choice was essentially something called *garam*, which was essentially rotten fish guts and rotten fish sauce. This was the salt, the principal seasoning ingredient, all across Europe. So even our own tastes have changed.

I think the last, for a lot of people, the last frontier is the textural thing. Particularly in Asia, they like squishy, or even rubbery, chewy, or a lot of traditional European cultures, you know, cartilage texture—that's something we really have a problem with. We tend to like crispy. Once you cross that border, you're really someplace special.

To get back to your question about delicacies, you've got to ask always, is there an assumed medical component to what we're talking about also? I think a lot of what we consider the really freakiest foods, the eye-popping, what the, why would you eat that—a lot of that has either folk medicine, or traditional Chinese medicine applications, or they're . . . You know, a regular feature of my life in China is if something arrives still wriggling, or there's a sex organ involved, it's usually accompanied by winking and banging on the bottom of the table, and someone saying, "This will make you strong," you know, "many, many sons, you go home," and it's like, oh God . . .

DEGRASSE TYSON: Tell me about these diets—we call them diets, but it's just the mainstay culinary offerings in various parts of the world. There's a lot spoken of the Mediterranean diet, or the Japanese diet, and they live a long time, heart disease is low . . . From your life experience, is all that true?

BOURDAIN: No doubt about it. You go to Crete, for instance—

DEGRASSE TYSON: Well I guess we know it's true, but are we going to credit the food, or because there's no stress? How big a factor is the food?

BOURDAIN: I'm guessing, you're a Vietnamese rice farmer, you're working hard. You are working hard. And there is stress in your life. Especially if you've been through three or four wars in the last thirty years. I don't think that's it. I think clearly the ratio, in much of the world—you know, I'm a confirmed carnivore, but clearly there's something to be said for cultures where the ratio of meat, of protein, to fresh vegetables is completely different. Ours—

DEGRASSE TYSON: The opposite.

BOURDAIN:—is distorted. Much of the cultures we're talking about, they use meat or bone or protein almost as a flavoring ingredient. Very carefully, much more valued.

DEGRASSE TYSON: A condiment, almost.

BOURDAIN: You have delicious—for the most part—vegetables, generally a filler like starch, whether it's rice or cassava or potatoes. Wherever it is, clearly it has an impact on what your body looks like and how long you're going to live. No doubt about it.

DEGRASSE TYSON: Now, you're over six feet tall. In Japan people hardly ever get to that height. So is it a tradeoff between that kind of diet and whether you grow tall?

BOURDAIN: Well, I don't think it's a tradeoff we make anymore, because they're getting taller and bigger, there's no doubt about it, as they become fonder of Western food and processed food. I mean, the same thing is happening there as here: the bulking of the world. But I think yeah, there clearly is.

I mean, one of my favorite—you know, I'm not particularly well inclined—as much as it might be good to eat more vegetables and less animal protein, I'm not particularly well-inclined toward really hardcore, unwavering vegans. So one of my favorite statistics is that apparently vegans in non-industrialized cultures seem to do much better than vegans in industrialized cultures. And people were trying to figure out why that was, why they were living longer and seemed healthier. [*Laughing*] Apparently the insect parts and carcasses in rice are much higher than in non-industrial cultures.

DEGRASSE TYSON: It's left in the product?

BOURDAIN: Yeah. So, basically, they're getting a lot more animal protein.

DEGRASSE TYSON: [*Laughing*] Insect protein. We're flicking away the insects out of our vegetables.

BOURDAIN: Very high in protein, bugs, by the way. People eat those for a reason.

DEGRASSE TYSON: What do you think of all the gadgets that help people cook food? Like great infomercials?

BOURDAIN: In almost every case they're completely worthless. "The Salad Shooter: The Ultimate Salad Delivery System." I mean, is cutting lettuce so hard? Something that will cut onions for you is completely insane, as far as I'm concerned. Two good knives—a serrated knife for bread, and maybe tomatoes, and a good quality chef's knife—is all you need. And a cutting board, a couple of good, heavyweight pans, and there is very little that you can't do.

DEGRASSE TYSON: How do you distinguish between tricks—and I don't mean it in a circus sense, but just se-crets—versus ten years of doing it? You serve a food to some-one and they say, "what's your secret?" as though they can just tell that to them and then tomorrow they can do exactly what you made. At what point do you say, "Look, I've been at this my whole life"?

BOURDAIN: There are no secrets. The secret of the restaurant business and professional cooking is there are no secrets. It is a mentoring business. Chefs spend their whole lives learning stuff, and then, because of the nature of the business, every few months teach everything they know, invest time they don't have, in teaching somebody everything they know so that they can maybe have a Sunday off, and that they can count on a crew. It is a military hierarchy, and it is import—there are no secrets. There are no secret recipes. There are no secret tech-niques. Everything that you learn in a kitchen you are either told, open-source, by your immediate superior and that's been shared with everybody in the kitchen, or you have learned it over time, painfully. You know, the ability to tell when a steak is cooked by listening to it in the pan or on the grill. Or determining that a piece of fish is probably ready to come out of the pan just from the sound of it—these are things you learn through repetition. And that is the great secret. It's that this is how professionals learn, this is how home cooks should learn. People shouldn't be intimidated by recipes. They should understand that professionals learn through getting it wrong, getting it wrong, getting it wrong, getting it wrong, start-ing to get it right, eventually getting it right, until it became second nature. It's repetition, repetition, repetition. You learn all of these things, even if you don't understand the technical, the science behind why your stew is transforming, why it's becoming thick as it cooks longer, why your egg scrambles, why the steak gets dark on the outside when you expose it to heat. You may have no understanding of the science behind that, but you instinctively—of course through repetition—understand it, you learn to use it, and you count on it.

DEGRASSE TYSON: Now, you've used two words in our conversation as fluently as any scientist that I know. First, "E. Coli" just rolled off your tongue.[*]

BOURDAIN: Yep.

DEGRASSE TYSON: And "tectonic shift" rolled off your tongue. [*Both laugh*] So what is your science background?

BOURDAIN: High school science.

DEGRASSE TYSON: High school science? Cool. But you liked it, I guess?

BOURDAIN: I did. But, you know, people talk about things in kitchens, like "what's happening, why is my steak getting brown?" The caramelization of protein, the Maillard reaction[†]—it's kind of cool to know. It helps you out to understand.

---

[*] Tyson is apparently referring to conversation that took place off camera.

[†] The Maillard reaction is the chemical reaction behind the browning of meats, breads, etc., which is the reaction between amino acids and reducing sugars.

DEGRASSE TYSON: I'm betting you didn't learn the caramel-ization of sugars in high school chemistry.

BOURDAIN: No, we learned it real quick—the first time you stick your figure in some, you learn it on a cellular level. How come that's hotter than water? I hadn't counted on that.

DEGRASSE TYSON: It's way hot.

• • •

DEGRASSE TYSON: Maybe it's more true in America than in other places, but we shield ourselves from—particularly in the carnivorous realm—we shield ourselves from the animal itself. We buy a chicken, you don't see the feet. You don't see the head. You know? It's just packaged, and it's just a piece of meat. Is that a good thing? You're probably going to say it's a bad thing—

BOURDAIN: No, it's a terrible thing.

DEGRASSE TYSON: But why? Why do you even care?

BOURDAIN: Okay. For a whole lot of reasons. It's always good to know where your food came from. It's only fair and just. My friend Fergus Henderson* was a pioneer of what's called the "nose to tail" movement. He says, it's only polite. If you are going to kill an animal—or, more often, have an

---

* An English chef known for his St. John restaurant in London, and his use of offal, and his philosophy of nose to tail eating.

animal killed—for your restaurant or your kitchen, it's only polite to eat as much of it as possible, to not waste. People should understand where their food comes from, how it was raised, what the impact might be on society as a whole in that process. But I think also, just as sentient, caring people, a decent person would prefer that their animal is raised reasonably happy and killed with a minimum of cruelty.

DEGRASSE TYSON: But if before everyone ordered their cowboy steak, if they said, "Go outside, find the cow that you want us to slaughter, look it in the eye, and pull this trigger and shoot it in its head—"

BOURDAIN: Honestly, I think that's an experience . . . the more people who can do—

DEGRASSE TYSON: A cow with big eyelashes, you know.

BOURDAIN: It is something I've done. You know, when you travel this world, you meet your dinner frequently. It's difficult. When you've killed your first pig, you really start to abhor waste, disrespect to the ingredient . . . I'm a lot more careful about how I cook my pork now, you know? I understand something died for that pork chop, okay? I think that you become a better citizen of the world and a more rounded person when you have seen that process and you've made some personal decisions as part of that. But it is a life-changing thing and I think that everyone should take part in it.

DEGRASSE TYSON: Some pathogens in our culture are directly traceable to viruses that hopped from animals that we either farm or eat. Does that scare you sometimes? I'm thinking of avian flu, or mad cow disease, or even AIDS, with contact with the rest of the apes.

BOURDAIN: I think exercising reasonable caution, the same way you would if you travel around rural America, is a useful thing to do wherever you go. The days when I would eat as far out of my comfort zone as a daredevil, just so that I could tell friends that I drank live cobra blood, I don't do that anymore, and I guess I would advise people against it.

DEGRASSE TYSON: But you used to do it?

BOURDAIN: Early on, I was so grateful to be traveling, I didn't think this whole TV thing would last, I'd never been anywhere . . . So yeah, when I was in Vietnam I made sure to get the live, still-beating cobra heart and drink its blood, just so I figured when it all ended six months later, at least I'd get a free beer telling that story, you know? Long ago I changed the way I travel to be much more interested in the typical, everyday thing. I think if you use the same philosophy—people always ask me, do you get sick, just stomach problems from traveling around and eating all that street food—always ask yourself: is this how your average person eats? Is the place busy? It's generally not going to be a concern. If you're aware that avian flu has become a concern in the area, yeah, undercooked poultry is probably not going to be a good idea, you will have to think about those things. If there's mad cow around, you know, maybe calves' brains at a dodgy pub would not be your first option. But I think if you familiarized yourself with what's going on, as any cautious traveler should, and don't take unreasonable risks—you know, eating brains or spine in a mad cow area would be a bad idea.

DEGRASSE TYSON: Using common sense.

BOURDAIN: Yeah. Just like they're not drinking water in Russia from the tap, you shouldn't either. [*Both laugh*]

DEGRASSE TYSON: Do as the natives do.

• • •

DEGRASSE TYSON: Later this afternoon I'm going to be speaking with the space station astronauts and I'm going to ask them—in part inspired by this conversation—I'm going to ask them, since it is an international space station, do they ever get together and swap each others' foods?

BOURDAIN: Well, they do. I've spoken to some astronauts about this and it's really interesting what happens to the palate at altitude and in outer space. Apparently, if you have a stash of hot sauce, you're the go-to guy in outer space. They crave spice, like chili sauce, tabasco, some kind of good spicy, relish seasoning . . .

DEGRASSE TYSON: Something to keep in mind. Our next mission to Mars, would you volunteer to be their chef? Or to advise NASA on it?

BOURDAIN: I'd really be interested in going to Mars. But nah, I ain't cooking. I had twenty-eight years of it. Somebody else can bring the food. I'll bring the hot sauce. [*Both laugh*]

DEGRASSE TYSON: You can be the spice man, I guess. How to make the food better.

BOURDAIN: You know, airline food tastes so differently on the ground and at altitude. They have to completely reimagine it for what it's going to taste like up there. So, given my experience in southeast Asia, I think I'd be a good choice for the master of condiments. [*Laughing*]

ANTHONY BOURDAIN TALKS TRAVEL, FOOD, AND WAR

INTERVIEW WITH JOHN W. LITTLE
BLOGS OF WAR
JULY 20, 2014

I've never met anyone interested in the world around them who isn't terribly envious of Anthony Bourdain. Fans of his books and shows like *No Reservations* and *Parts Unknown* know that he is far more than a roving chef. He is a keen observer of the human condition who leverages mankind's shared passion for a well-cooked meal as a tool of discovery. In over a decade of circling the globe he has seen the best and worst that humanity has to offer and he has seen it in more places than the vast majority of us could ever hope to visit. This broad experience, and the ability to think deeply about the world around him, truly sets him apart. It's also why interviewing him for *Blogs of War* is an absolute no-brainer.

JOHN W. LITTLE: So I would not be surprised if some readers are confused by your appearance on a war blog, but conflict, history, geography, and food are intimately related aren't they?

ANTHONY BOURDAIN: I wouldn't have thought so when I first set out traveling the world with nothing, really, on my mind but shoving food in my face, but right away—very early on—I came to realize that everything, particularly something as intimate as a meal, is a reflection of both a place's history and its present political and military circumstances. In fact, the meal is where you can least escape the realities of a nation's situation. People tend to be less guarded and more frank (particularly when alcohol is involved). What you are eating is always the end of a very long story—and often an ingenious but delicious answer to some very complicated problems. Within months of leaving the professional kitchen for what turned out to be a non-stop voyage around the world, I found myself in the Mekong delta sitting down and getting hammered with a group of former VC. The senior member of the group was a very old dude, who when I asked if he felt any animosity towards me, towards my country, why he was being so damned nice, laughed in my face and started ticking off all the other countries he'd fought in his time: Chinese, French, Japanese, Cambodians, Chinese again. He basically said, "don't flatter yourself that you were anything special—now drink!" When you travel with no agenda other than asking the simple questions, sharing a moment with people around the table, people tell you extraordinary things. You tend to notice things that can't be avoided. The guy cooking dinner for me near the Plain of Jars in Laos was missing a few limbs. It was worth asking how that happened. The answer—though simple—tends in such circumstances—to lead to very complicated back stories. In this case, a simple question with a very long and frankly fascinating answer (our enormous secret war in Laos).

But finding myself in Beirut during the 2006 war was

clearly a defining moment for the show—and some kind of crossroads for me personally. To stand there, day after day, useless and relatively safe by a hotel pool, looking at the people and the neighborhoods I had just been getting to know being hammered back twenty years a few short miles away was . . . well . . . it was something. And the complete disconnect between what I was seeing and hearing on the ground from Beirutis of all stripes and what was being reported was something that stuck with me. Beirut is such a fantastic city—a place of such unbelievable possibilities. You can be sitting by the pool or listening to techno in a club one minute and having a wary conversation with Hezbollah ten minutes later. It's a very short ride. For all its problems (all the problems and all the evils in the world in miniature, basically), it's an absolutely magical, gorgeous city. Impossible to not fall in love with. It's pheromonic. Some cities just smell good the second you land.

After Beirut, there was a conscious effort to tell more complicated stories. We realized that when you ask people "What do you like to eat? What do you like to cook? What makes you happy?" and are willing to spend the time necessary to hear the answers, that you are often let "in" in ways that a hard news reporter working a story might not be. So I've been able to look at places like post-Benghazi Libya, the DRC, Liberia, Haiti, Cuba, Gaza, the West Bank, Kurdistan and recently Iran from a very intimate angle. Those are all very long stories, and if you don't take that time to listen, to take in the everyday things—the things that happened before the news story—there's not much hope in understanding them.

An interesting thing we noticed a while back was when

we were shooting in pre-revolution Egypt. When we expressed a desire to shoot a segment at one of the ubiquitous street stands selling fūl,* our fixers and translators, who, no doubt also worked for some sinister department of the Interior Ministry, were absolutely adamant that we not do it. What was it about this simple, everyday, working class meal of beans and flatbread that just about everyone in Cairo was eating that was so threatening? Turns out, they knew better than us. The price of bread had been going up. The army controlled most of the bakeries and stocks of flour. There had been riots over bread elsewhere in the country. And the inescapable fact was that fūl was *all* that much of the population was eating and the bastards knew it. That was an image they apparently considered sensitive, dangerous: their countrymen eating bread.

If you're going to shoot in a place like the Congo, you can't just show up and ask what's for dinner—it's essential to know the history. It's so central to everything you see and experience. It hangs over everything, practically suffocates it at times. "Why are things like this?" You need at least a clue. You have to read up before you even think about going. (In my case, Congo has been a decades long obsession). Otherwise you'll look like an idiot. Or worse, find yourself in some serious shit.

Some environments, like Libya, its nice to know the history but events on the ground change so quickly it almost doesn't matter. You have to develop a whole new style of moving and adapting. You learn as you go. And you learn fast.

---

*   Stewed fava beans with a variety of herbs and spices including cumin, garlic, onion, lemon juice and chilies.

LITTLE: Your work has taken you to more parts of the world than most of us could ever hope to see. Is it difficult to reconcile the hospitality you receive on your travels and the commonality of experience we have with food with the brutal reality we see around us every day?

BOURDAIN: It is a constant series of surprises, of having everything I thought I knew turned upside down. People nearly everywhere have been lovely to me. Most places, people are extremely proud of their food and are frankly flattered when somebody asks about it. Palestinians in particular seemed delighted that someone—anyone—would care to depict them eating and cooking and doing normal, everyday things—you know, like people do. They are so used to camera crews coming in to just get the usual shots of rock-throwing kids and crying women.

I used to think that basically, the whole world, that all humanity were basically bastards. I've since found that most people seem to be pretty nice—basically good people doing the best they can. There is rarely, however, a neat takeaway. You have to learn to exercise a certain moral relativity, to be a good guest first—as a guiding principle. Otherwise you'd spend the rest of the world lecturing people, pissing people off, confusing them and learning nothing. Do I pipe up every time my Chinese host serves me some cute animal I may not approve of? Should I inquire of my Masai buddies if they still practice female genital mutilation? Express revulsion in Liberia over tribal practices?

Fact is, the guy who's been patting my knee all night, telling jokes, sharing favorite *Seinfeld* anecdotes, making sure

I get the best part of the lamb, being my new bestest buddy in Saudi Arabia will very likely later, on the drive back to the hotel, guilelessly express regret over what "the Jews and the CIA" did to my city on 9/11. What do you say to that? Or in Anatolia, the Kurdish religious elders there who asked me for reassurance that "Obama is indeed a Muslim, yes?" I hated to disappoint them. So I didn't. My first obligation, I feel, is to be a good guest. I go to great lengths, and have had to choke down some pretty funky meals to do that. Its a strategy I highly recommend if you're looking to make friends and have a good conversation. Sometimes you have to take one for the team but its well worth it.

Iran was mind-blowing. My crew has *never* been treated so well—by total strangers everywhere. We had heard that Persians are nice. But nic*est*? Didn't see that coming. Its very confusing. Total strangers thrilled to encounter Americans, just underneath the inevitable "Death To America" mural. The gulf between perception and reality, between government policy and what you see on the street and encounter in people's homes, in restaurants—everywhere—it's just incredible. There's no way to be prepared for it.

Trying to reconcile the very real consequences of Iranian foreign and national policy with the way Iran is internally and who is actually living there, how old they are, what they actually want and believe in. *Very* confusing.

It's easier to think of Iran as a monolith—in an uncomplicated, ideological way. More comfortable, too. Life ain't that simple. It *is* complicated. And filled with nuance worth exploring.

A constant on my travels is nice, incredibly hospitable people, often very reasonable people. Unfortunately, another constant is that nice, reasonable people are being ground under the wheel.

LITTLE: You visited Gaza and the West Bank in season two of your show *Parts Unknown*. You showed a rare ability to find hope and tragedy on all sides. Did filming that episode change your view of the Israeli-Palestinian conflict in any way? On a personal level does that awareness lead anywhere positive or do you just find yourself hopelessly conflicted?

BOURDAIN: It's impossible to see Gaza, for instance, the camps, the West Bank and not find yourself reeling with the ugliness of it all. The absolute failure of smart, presumably good-hearted people on both sides to find something/ anything better than what we've arrived at. And the willingness of people to not see what is plainly apparent, right there, enormous and frankly, hideous. Unfortunately, we live in a world where it's nearly impossible to even describe reality much less deal with it. It's utterly heartbreaking.

LITTLE: Your introduction to that show really resonated with me. You said "There's no hope, none, of ever talking about it without pissing somebody, if not everybody, off . . . By the end of this hour I will be seen by many as a terrorist sympathizer, a Zionist tool, a self-hating Jew, an apologist for American imperialism, an orientalist, socialist, fascist, CIA agent, and worse." Unfortunately, this is a typical day for me on Twitter. The inability to have an honest public discussion about this conflict without facing virulent attacks from all sides only perpetuates the tragedy doesn't it? Was the inevitable blow-back cause for any trepidation on your part or did you just charge in?

BOURDAIN: I thought about how I was going to do a show in the region for a very long time. And yes, there was a lot of trepidation. And I knew there would be recriminations and unhappiness no matter what I did or said or showed. But ultimately, I decided to just say, fuck it and take it head on. Frankly, it was much better received than I could ever have expected. The reaction from the Arab and Palestinian community was overwhelmingly positive—which I found both flattering and dismaying. I say dismaying because I did so little. I showed so little. It seems innocuous. But it was apparently a hell of a lot more than what they are used to seeing on Western television. For some, unfortunately, depicting Palestinians as anything other than terrorists is proof positive that you have an agenda, that you have bought in to some sinister propaganda guidelines issuing from some evil central command in charge of interfacing with Western com/symp dupes. A photo of a Palestinian washing their car or playing with their child is, therefore automatically "propaganda."

I recently retweeted a photo of two dead children on the beach in Gaza. I had walked on that same beach. The photo (which later appeared on the front page of *The New York Times*) was taken from—or near—the same hotel I had stayed in. I am the father of a seven year old girl who I, of course, adore. I retweeted the picture with the comment that as a father, as someone who had walked that beach, I felt particularly horrified. That's all I said. The reaction? This was not, it would seem a "Oh, yeah? well, what about . . . ?" situation. The photo did not require, one would think, any equivalency, a countervailing argument. It's a picture of dead children. Period. The appropriate reaction, one would think would be "How terrible!" But, as it turned out, of course, even this image would be hijacked by extremists of both sides, the conversation devolving into ugly racist shit and accusations.

This is all too often the world we live in now—where even a simple, heartfelt, human reaction—the kind of emotion any father would have—is tantamount to choosing sides.

If I have a side, its against extremism—of any kind: religious, political, other: there's no conversation when everybody is absolutely certain of the righteousness of their argument. That's a platitude. But it's still true.

LITTLE: So you told me in a previous exchange that you're a bit of an espionage geek. You are fascinated by KGB defector Yuri Nosenko and you have picked mushrooms with Victor Cherkashin (the KGB counterintelligence officer who ran Aldrich Ames and Robert Hanssen). With all the travel, contacts you make, and fixers you employ I imagine that there must be more than a few moments where you and your crew cross paths with intelligence officials and spies. Does it ever get interesting? And as a frequent traveler, observer, writer, and relationship builder do you find that you share a lot of common ground with intelligence professionals?

BOURDAIN: Sometimes it's charming. Often it's not. Often our fixers in a Communist country, for instance, will, after a few drinks, fess up. Basically they will admit they work for the intelligence service and will ask earnestly that we do whatever the hell we want as long as we don't embarrass them or make them look bad. They're supposed to be watching us, but chances are, they have people watching them too. We try to be sensitive to that. We are who we say we are. Our "agenda" is exactly what we said it was. So it's usually not difficult.

I've actually become good friends over the years with some of them. And it's something we always have to think about: I can go back home and say whatever I want about my experiences in China, for instance. But the people who trusted us, hung out with us, helped us while we there—they remain. There can be consequences to what I end up saying on TV. Not for me. For the people who were with us while in country. I try, as best I can, to be sensitive to that. I'm not looking to put anybody in the soup. Even if they were spying on me. They are, after all, just doing their job.

I like grey areas, obviously. I like ambiguity (the Nosenko case being a terrific example) and tend to enjoy the company of people who deal in ambiguity. Victor Cherkashin. Nice guy. Great host, lunch companion. A man who has done— what we would certainly describe as many bad things. I feel the same way about Ted Nugent. I don't have to agree with a guy to enjoy their company. As a political ideology and as a practical matter, I loathe communism. However, I often find myself getting along very well with communists. I feel the same way about Red State America. Not my world, not always my point of view. But I always have a good time in gun country America and tend to like the people I meet. Palin sticker on your bumper or Che Guevara—if you have a sense of humor and enjoy food made with pride, chances are, we can be pals.

I assume I share one characteristic with a good case officer: empathy. I'm good at looking at things from the other guy's point of view. I can put myself in their shoes. I'm willing to reach out. I'm a good listener. The overlap pretty much ends there.

Convincing some poor slob to betray his country, though—which is pretty much the job of the spook—is something I'd never have the stomach for.

ANTHONY BOURDAIN ON FOOD: THERE IS NOTHING MORE POLITICAL

INTERVIEW WITH PETER ARMSTRONG
CBC NEWS *ON THE MONEY*
NOVEMBER 7, 2016

PETER ARMSTRONG: Well thank you so much for coming in. It's great to see you. To what extent is food the best or maybe least biased glimpse into how a society, a country, an economy works?

ANTHONY BOURDAIN: Well there's nothing more political. There's nothing more revealing of the real situation on the ground, whether a system works or not. I mean, whatever your philosophical, uh, the foundation of your personal belief system, it's difficult to spend time in Cuba, particularly like ten years ago, eat with ordinary people, and come out of it thinking "Wow, this system is really working out for everybody." [*Armstrong laughs*] Who gets to eat, who doesn't get to eat, what they're eating—I mean, the food itself on the plate is usually the end result of a very long and often very painful story. I mean, is there a lot of food preservation, is there a lot of pickling? You know, certain countries, their cuisine very much reflects either a siege mentality, or abundance, or intermittent periods of difficulty. Also people just—if you go in not as a journalist but just as someone who's asking simple questions like, "What do you like to eat? What makes you happy?" people tend to drop their defenses and tell you extraordinary things that are very revealing.

ARMSTRONG: And where do you get this stuff—I mean, the production chain, and how you get all this food, tells you so much about how an economy functions, doesn't it?

BOURDAIN: Well, I think maybe the strongest example that snuck up on us when we were shooting in Egypt before the Arab Spring, we wanted to shoot a scene with fūl, which is the everyday food of working-class Cairo. And our fixers and local translators suddenly were all up in arms. "No no no, you must not shoot this. You can't shoot fūl." I said, "Wait, it's ubiquitous, it's everywhere. It's not interesting." We said, "No, we'd really like to shoot it." They said "It's forbidden. We'll kick you out."

We ended up getting the shot anyway through various devious strategies, but I think what they were concerned about was they understood that it's not just typical, it's *all there is to eat.* And the army controlled, I guess, the flour supply, there'd been bread riots. And they were not so much worried about how it would look outside of the country, but the show is aired within the country, and I don't think they wanted their own people seeing it. Particularly after an episode of the same show shot in France.

ARMSTRONG: You fly into a country—especially for this show—you're trying to sort of understand a new place, you're trying to explain a new place to viewers like us. When you go to a place for the first time, you get off the plane, you go downtown, do you go high-end food? Do you go street meat?

BOURDAIN: No, it's what's most typical. A good starting point is always the market, early morning markets. See what's seasonal, what's available, what people are buying. Also there are usually little food stalls that are serving people who work in the market. People talk to you in environments like that, generally in a good mood, open to try out their English if that's interesting to them. Yeah, I'm not interested in high-end restaurants in general. Unless it's something really unusual and extraordinary and new that says something in and of itself. That there's an emerging haut-cuisine in Mexico, for instance, that's really interesting to me. But generally speaking, no, that's not what I'm looking at first.

ARMSTRONG: And again, the markets sort of help you understand—you know, we were talking about Gaza off-air—that it's the fishing is the primary thing, you know, the fish are coming in, that's how people are making their living, that's how people are, sort of, trading and making their way in the world.

BOURDAIN: But, you know, as soon as you're at the fish market—well, they're getting their fish two ways. Within the one mile—I think it's a mile limit—because if they go beyond a mile they risk getting their boat sunk. Or through the tunnels from Egypt. Already, the subject is fraught with peril. It's extremely controversial. But it's the sort of thing that, on my show, I get the comment to "Stick with food, man. We don't want to hear politics from you. You're a chef, you know, shut up, we don't want your political opinion." Okay, fair enough, but it's difficult to not notice the elephant in the room. "How come you only have these fish?" "Well, we can't go any further out to sea." You know, "How come you're missing two of your limbs in Laos?" "Well, you know, when I was a little boy, I was walking around in a field and stepped on one of the eight million tons of ordnance you guys left in my country." Look, those are inescapable facts. How you choose to feel about them or interpret them, is up to you.

ARMSTRONG: And your audience, certainly on the television show, has come to expect that, and to really sort of appreciate that it's this guided tour that isn't a political documentary about a world, but it's a glimpse into a society. Is the book a similar vein, that you get to learn more about a place by cooking and by experiencing?

BOURDAIN: This is more of when I'm not out there in the world. This is the little place that I keep for myself. It's what I cook when I'm cooking for a nine year old and her friends, and when I'm cooking at home and sort of comforting myself and a few friends and family.

ARMSTRONG: You said in an interview I read a couple days ago that you've changed your take on brunch as a result of having a kid.

BOURDAIN: Well, I hated brunch because for many years of my life, for many low points in my professional career, when I was sort of unemployable by any reputable restaurant for various reasons, I could always get a brunch gig. Because restaurants are always desperate to find somebody to cook three hundred omelettes for drunks on Sunday morning, and that was me. And so the smell of eggs cooking and French toast was always the smell of shame and defeat and humiliation until I became a dad. And now, if I want the fast track to looking cool in front of my daughter's friends, it's make a pancake bar for them, you know, "Your choice: chocolate chip, blueberry, banana?"

ARMSTRONG: [*Laughing*] What fun you can have, huh?

BOURDAIN: Yeah.

ARMSTRONG: I want to talk a bit about the TV industry and where you started and where it's going now. You've been making these kinds of shows for a while and have had great success at them. What has changed over that period of time to where we are now?

BOURDAIN: Well I can only really tell you what changed for me. I think there are certain hard and fast rules of television. CNN, unlike everyone else I've ever worked for, have never called me up and started a conversation with "How about," or "Have you thought about," or "We've got an idea." I have complete and total autonomy. I'm privileged to be able to go out there and make whatever shows I want wherever I want with zero interference.

But I think my previous experiences with two other

networks are that everyone on television who works in the television industry by and large lives in fear. And what they're afraid of is that someday they won't be on television. So they're not gonna try anything new, because, well, they'll say they want something new, but what they really mean is the same thing that worked last year. Because they don't want to be the guy who's stuck out there having proposed something that doesn't work. Everybody kind of adheres to what worked last year. The engine of television on the creative side was always "Do what worked last week." Which is exactly the opposite of what interests me, which is to never repeat what I did last week, whether people liked it or not. But I'm kind of a freak in the business, in that a) I'm not interested in doing the same thing, even if it worked, and b) you know, it wouldn't be the worst thing in the world to not be on television anymore.

ARMSTRONG: That distance, I think, gives you great power in that relationship. But at the same time, does it give us a glimpse into where the art, the craft, and the business of television are going? There's a success in this, and that, you know—emulate it people, get out there, follow this.

BOURDAIN: It's a shrinking industry. It's an industry under tremendous pressure from the digital universe. And again, people are "We want something new and proactive and young and crazy and out there"—but not really.

ARMSTRONG: "We don't really want that."

BOURDAIN: "We want it to be just like what's working over there, only our own watered-down version." Or "We're just gonna step back and stick with what we know always works." And there are certain rules, particularly in the food travel space. You know, if you did every show of people shoving barbecue into their face, that's gonna be a hit show.

ARMSTRONG: My favorite quote about television was the old Hunter Thompson line about it's the "shallow money trench."* It is now, "If you're going to do something as undignified as making television, it should be fun." Which is a quote you gave to a colleague of mine at the *Globe and Mail* last week. Is it fun? Can you make television fun? And is that a sort of enduring lesson of making good television?

BOURDAIN: I don't know whether it's a lesson of making good television, but incredibly enough, it's worked for me. For me, the satisfaction of television is largely a technical one. It's about how can we do this show differently, how can we push ourselves creatively—not just me, but my camera guys, the post-production, the sound mixers and sound designers, the editors—how can we do something different? How can we outdo ourselves? How can we do something strange and wonderful that will confuse and terrify our network?

ARMSTRONG: Your show is largely about bridging cultures and learning more about someone else and somewhere else

---

* In his book *Generation of Swine,* Thompson said, "The TV business is uglier than most things. It is normally perceived as some kind of cruel and shallow money trench through the heart of the journalism industry, a long plastic hallway where thieves and pimps run free and good men die like dogs, for no good reason."

that maybe I'll never go, or maybe now as a result of watching it I'll get to go. Do you find yourself coming up on this growing sentiment of anti-immigration and xenophobia, these concerns about trade, the Trumps and Brexits, this rising sentiment in the world?

BOURDAIN: I bump into it a lot. Look, I think if you travel as long as I have and as much as I have, and you meet as many people and spend time with them in countries that we're supposed to hate and who are supposed to hate us, when you see how similar—and different, but mostly similar—people are, particularly when sitting around a table. It makes it very, very hard—when you see how the economies of the world are completely interdependent and interlocked, and the flow of money back and forth—it's hard to come back and not be horrified and dismayed by the willful, I mean *willful* ignorance of the kind of conversation we're having now, often by people who know better. You know, Trump has—so much of his interests rest abroad and are completely dependent on other countries. It's ludicrous for him to on one hand take this very xenophobic, protectionist point of view, that would make it impossible for his businesses to continue.

ARMSTRONG: Well, I'm afraid we have to leave it there, but thanks a lot for this conversation. It's been a fascinating conversation.

BOURDAIN: Thank you.

TELLING STORIES THROUGH FOOD ON *PARTS UNKNOWN*

INTERVIEW WITH TREVOR NOAH
THE DAILY SHOW WITH TREVOR NOAH
JANUARY 17, 2018

TREVOR NOAH: My guest tonight is a world-renowned chef, best-selling author and publisher, and host of the Emmy-winning CNN original series *Anthony Bourdain: Parts Unknown*. Please welcome, Anthony Bourdain!

[*Applause*]

Welcome to the show.

ANTHONY BOURDAIN: Thank you. Good to be here.

NOAH: I've been a fan of yours for so long, watching you travel around the world, and it was so amazing this week I guess it was, uh, perfect timing—CNN aired a bunch of your shows, Anthony Bourdain, specifically of you in Africa around the same time that the president was commenting on how these are "shithole countries."

BOURDAIN: Yeah, what a coincidence! [*Laughing*]

NOAH: Right. You tweeted about the president saying "shit-hole countries." Why did it affect you so much, why did it offend you so much?

BOURDAIN: Because apparently I've wasted my life going to shitholes. I mean, I've spent 17 years travelling around to extraordinary places. I mean, the notion that people don't work hard—clearly no one on his team has been to Nigeria, where people work like no one I've ever seen . . . It was just deeply, I mean, enraging, enraging to me because it's a refutation of everything I've seen, experienced, all the people I've met, and everything I've done in the past 17 years.

NOAH: Would you say that that's something that has shaped your experiences, and shaped your world-view—travelling to these places? Because, I mean, for many people, in their defense, they see images of Africa and they go "Oh, that place doesn't look great," but on your show you have gone to, as you say, parts unknown, some of the most beautiful locations and unlikely destinations. Does it change how you see the people and the places?

BOURDAIN: Yeah. I think Mark Twain said, that "travel is lethal to prejudice." You know, the extent to which you can walk in another person's shoes, to see how hard people work and struggle on a daily basis, even for very little . . . And the extent to which you see how much people *do,* how well things are going. I mean I love showing up in places thinking one thing, and having those expectations turned on their heads all the time. But then again, you know, I'm a fool. I think curiosity is a virtue [*laughing*] and that's not something, uh . . .

[*Applause*]

NOAH: Let me ask you this. Just like, on a food-level, as a chef . . . What do you think America would be like if there were no food, if there were no foods, from any of these other countries?

BOURDAIN: Well, to start with, good ol' American Southern food as we know it, you know, classic Americana, wouldn't exist. I mean, if you spend any time in Ghana, you see exactly where, you know, food that we tend to associate on Food Network with, you know, old white ladies, well, we learn this is African food!

[*Audience laughter*]

So, look, the history of the world is on your plate. Every plate of food is an expression of, often, a long struggle, a long story, and I guess that's one of the satisfactions, one of the joys of travelling and eating as you find out who's cooking, and why, and where these things come from. I mean, I grew up in the early sixties. American food then, your options were extremely limited. You know, so the more we have people from somewhere else bringing their food chain, and ingredients, and traditions—life only gets better.

NOAH: When you look at that statement, the food telling you a story about people, not just the people who are preparing it, but the people who are eating it, which I think is a beautiful statement, if someone was to eat cheeseburgers every day, all the time, what do you think that would say about them and their culinary tastes, as a person?

BOURDAIN: 239 pounds, apparently.*

[*Audience laughter and applause*]

You know I think it's worth noting, it is reported, that President Trump, in his year in Washington D.C, which is a very good restaurant town, has never been to any other restaurant than his steak house at the Trump Hotel—

NOAH: Where he eats well done steaks, with ketchup.

BOURDAIN: You're hurting me.

NOAH: I know, I know. I'm doing this on purpose

BOURDAIN: That hurts. I am interested, though. Do you think he can use chopsticks?

NOAH: That sounds like an insult . . . but it's a valid question.

---

* Donald Trump's physician had recently released the results of his examination of the President, claiming this was his weight, to derision from the press, which noted that Trump was obviously heavier than that.

BOURDAIN: I'd be curious to know.

NOAH: If that was, like, on the test to determine whether or not you could be president, I think America might be calling him President Pence right now. Let's move on and talk about the journey life has taken you on so far. *Anthony Bourdain: Parts Unknown* has taken you on many journeys. You know, you've grown as a person. One of the more painful, and I would think interesting journeys you've taken on your life just happened very recently in regards to the #MeTooMovement—

BOURDAIN: Mmm-hmm.

NOAH:—happening not just in America, but in many parts of the world. Your girlfriend was one of the people who first came out and exposed a story regarding Harvey Weinstein.

BOURDAIN: Mmm-hmm.

NOAH: Your comments posted were really interesting because not only were you supportive, you felt disappointed in yourself because there were many women you now heard stories from who didn't tell you the stories, and you regarded them as friends.

BOURDAIN: Yeah.

NOAH: Why were you disappointed in yourself?

BOURDAIN: Um . . . you know I came out of a brutal, oppressive business that was historically unfriendly to women. I knew a lot of women, it turned out, who had stories about their experiences about people I knew, who did not feel I was the sort of person they could confide in. And suddenly, because of my association with Asia, people were talking to me. And, in fact, I had started speaking about it. I have a sense of real rage. I mean, I'd like to say that I arrived, I was always enlightened in some way, or that I'm an activist, or I'm virtuous, but in fact, you know, I have to be honest with myself. I met one extraordinary woman with an extraordinary and painful story, who introduced me to a lot of other women with extraordinary stories, and suddenly it was personal. And that, that woke me to the extent I ever woke up, that certainly had an effect.

So, I think like a lot of men, I'm reexamining my life. I, you know, I wrote sort of the meathead Bible for uh, restaurant employees and chefs. And, you know, I look back like, I hope, a lot of men in that industry, and say, not so much what did I do or not do, but what did I see, and what did I let slide . . . what did I not notice? I think that's something people are really going to have to take into account now.

NOAH: Yeah, it is something the movement is definitely demanding of men in all industries. And I think what was particularly painful was you expressed it so honestly, you know, when Mario Batali's story came out, and then other chefs came out—these were people who you regarded as friends, and these are people who, you know, in a nuanced world people struggle to understand, may still be a friend. But-but how do you grapple with that? Like, how do you wrap your head around that? What do you aim to do going forward? Will you go, like, "As Anthony Bourdain, I have a platform, I have, you know, an imprint. I have access to this world, of chefs, of restaurants . . . " What do you aspire to now?

BOURDAIN: Well, it's been a long time since I've been in the— it's been about 20 years since I've been in the industry, and I have been removed from it. But, I mean, look, no matter how much I admire someone, or respected their work, you know, I'm pretty much Mean the Merciless on this issue right now. You know, I'm not in a forgiving state of mind. I mean, that shit ain't okay.

[Audience applause and cheering]

NOAH: The business that you are in now involves not just travelling around the world, but helping people of diverse backgrounds have a voice writing cookbooks, telling their stories about their parts that are unknown. You, Anthony Bourdain, you could have just done it for yourself. Why was it so important for you to get these people involved, and to help them get their stories out there?

BOURDAIN: Um, you know, I'm one of those annoying peo- ple, if I read a book, or see a movie, or listen to a record I really, really like, If I could I'd come over to your house and shove it in your hands, and sit there and you know, listen to it with you to make sure you don't miss anything, or re-read every line, you know?

NOAH: That is an annoying person. [*Laughing*] Yeah, I know those people.

BOURDAIN: I'm passionate to the point of being evangelical about things that I love, that give me pleasure, and make me excited. And, um, you know I didn't really travel until I was forty-two years old, I spent my whole life in kitchens. I'd seen nothing of the world. So, this is all still relatively new to me. People have been very kind to me. I feel very, very, very fortunate. So as a publisher, as somebody who puts people from all over the world on television, you know, to a great extent it is a selfish act because I'm having fun, I enjoy it, it makes me feel good. But I'm also, um, coming to as many people's houses as possible, and sitting down next to them, and watching the movie next to them and saying, you know, I want you to notice this. I want you to see how awesome these places are. I don't feel like I'm an advocate, or a spokesperson for *anything*. I'm just, you know, I'm an enthusiastic son of a bitch. And I'm having a really good time, and the things that make me happy, uh, you know, especially if I feel it's somebody who's not reaching a wider audience, well I'd like to help.

NOAH: I love that, man. Anthony Bourdain, "enthusiastic son of a bitch." Thank you so much for being on the show.

BOURDAIN: Thank you.

NOAH: Anthony Bourdain, everybody!

THE LAST INTERVIEW: ANTHONY BOURDAIN ON ASIA ARGENTO, HIS FAVORITE MOVIES, AND WHY DONALD TRUMP WOULD BE A TERRIBLE DINNER COMPANION

INTERVIEW WITH ERIC KOHN
INDIEWIRE
JUNE 3, 2018

Anthony Bourdain watched thirty minutes of *Baby Driver* before he walked out of the movie theater. "It rubbed me the wrong way from the beginning," he said, looking back on an experience that led him to tweet "Fuck BABY DRIVER" to his millions of followers. "I felt like right away I knew what was going to happen to everybody in the cast. I just felt it was telegraphed so early and painfully. I had a violent physical reaction. I stumbled out the theater in a pit of depression and fury."

That's the thing about Bourdain, who has spent two decades hosting food shows with a unique blend of machismo, travel fever, and cultural inquiry: A television personality who's a creature of cinema, he devours movies almost as frequently as the cuisines at the center of his show. And in all instances, he's man of discerning tastes.

"When you called, I was watching *Edge of Darkness*, with Mel Gibson, which is this horrifyingly bad film based on this incredibly great five-hour British series," he said, picking up the phone on a Thursday afternoon in between shoots. "I'm mesmerized by its awfulness. Some things should never be remade."

That said, Bourdain often indulges in remakes and homages within his shows. On CNN's *Anthony Bourdain: Parts Unknown*, which he's hosted for five years, his cinematic influences often overshadow the food in the various countries he travels. "It's always been, to one extent or another, a stealth food show," he said. "We pretend it's about food. It rarely is. We always talk about films first, before we head to a location, for visual cues, for sound, for editing. We love nothing more than duping, emulating, or riffing on a film that few of our audiences have actually seen."

A PERFECT MATCH

On his show, Bourdain has spent time with film luminaries ranging from Frances Ford Coppola to Darren Aronofsky, but the June 3 episode is an especially potent reflection of his cinephilia: "Hong Kong" finds Bourdain celebrating the city through his longtime affection for Wong Kar-wai movies, sampling expressionistic clips from *Chungking Express* and *In the Mood for Love*, and hanging around the city with the filmmaker's rambunctious cinematographer Christopher Doyle. Watching Doyle, a kooky ball of energy whose grey hair and lanky figure resemble Bourdain enough to make them look like brothers, it's a wonder it took so long for their paths to cross. "He was a hero to me," Bourdain said. "I had hoped and planned to just do a couple of scenes with the guy, talk about his films, how he looked at Hong Kong, what he looked for there."

Instead, Doyle zipped around Hong Kong with Bourdain and his crew, talking through his creative philosophy and introducing him to various locals. Ultimately, Doyle took charge of the camerawork—in the show, he arrives late to one restaurant sit-down and forces the team to redo the setup—and served as one of three credited cinematographers. "It was this wonderful, magical sort of kismet," Bourdain said.

Speaking to the host as they roam the city, Doyle expresses a series of philosophies that resonate with Bourdain's own. "Our job as artists is to show you the world you think you know and celebrate it," the camera guru says at one point, later adding, "If we try to be as true as possible to the way we see things, perhaps, perhaps, it translates [and] gives voice to the unspoken."

The forty-two-minute episode celebrates Wong and Doyle's work, but in a broader sense, it feels like a natural extension of Bourdain's homegrown oeuvre—it's a lush, riveting overview of Hong Kong's history, its struggles with gentrification, and multicultural inhabitants. They just happen to be eating great food, too.

The episode also points to another new collaborator in Bourdain's life: Actress and filmmaker Asia Argento, Bourdain's girlfriend, served as a last-minute director when the original director fell ill. (The couple first met when Argento appeared on the show's eighth season in 2016.)

It's a welcome new chapter for Argento, who has spent months contending with being one of several victims of sexual abuse by Harvey Weinstein to speak out about it. With the episode airing a week after Weinstein's courtroom arraignment, Argento declined to be interviewed about her experience on the show, but in an official Q&A posted to CNN's site, she said she "happily made this leap into the unknown," and noted that her experience acting in Olivier Assayas' 2007 Hong Kong thriller *Boarding Gate* prepared her for the challenge of running around the city with a camera. "I felt a kinship with the organized chaos," she said.

For Bourdain, bringing Argento further into his professional world proved to be a natural extension of their bond. "Look, anytime I can get work out of Asia, even random suggestions, like when she calls me mid-show to make me aware of a Nigerian psychedelic rock scene of the mid-to-late-'70s— that's a huge help to the show," he said. "I'd love to have her a continuing director. I just don't think we can afford her. But, my god, I'd love nothing more than to repeat the experience. She made it incredible."

Argento's own work on both sides of the camera tends toward rough, visceral narrative experiences, and her sensibilities prove a natural union with Bourdain, whose baritone voiceover and John Wayne swagger sits at the cross-section of Hong Kong's evolving identity. From a swift overview of the city's growth from a fishing village into a global center of urban development, the episode careens through beguiling locations: upscale cantonese eatery Happy Paradise, a grimy punk rock club where he dines with a young band named David Boring, tranquil boat rides, and a Ghanaian restaurant for African refugees.

Doyle frequently usurps Bourdain's penchant for poetic observations. Considering the impact of construction and rising costs of living for the city's older population, Doyle asserts, "We can't change the evolution of history or gentrification—but at least we can see what we're losing." He's joined by filmmaker Jenny Suen, who co-directed *The White Girl* with Doyle last year. Suen's perspective rescues the episode from the lingering possibility of an Orientalist simplification. In considering the challenges of representing the culture for non-Chinese audiences, she concludes, "The only way is not to be cynical about it."

AN INQUISITIVE SPIRIT

This has been Bourdain's own ethos as he has settled into his groove. "I'm there to listen," he said, reflecting on a scene in the episode where an African man notes over one meal that he has been stuck in Hong Kong ever since the Trump Administration's travel ban has prevented him from traveling to the U.S. "I don't go in asking hard-news questions, but incredibly enough, again and again, just by sitting down with people over food and giving them a platform where I can listen to them, they say extraordinary things that can be very political in their implications." He pointed to an episode last year, set in Laos, where he dines with the victim of American attacks during the Vietnam war. "It's obscene to sit there enjoying a platter of half chicken when somebody in the room with you has been injured by landmines or American explosives," he said.

Though he's an outspoken critic of many issues in his public life, Bourdain has tip-toed around politics for much of his show, with the exception of the current season opener in West Virginia. "I went into West Virginia with a political agenda in the sense that I wanted to go in and just let people

speak for themselves," he said, referring to the Trump sup-
porters in the program. "I wanted to give them a break in
spite of any preconceptions I might have had."

However, while he shared a beer with Barack Obama
last season in Hanoi, Bourdain sees no potential to bring the
current president onto his program. "I talked to President
Obama as a father, as a parent, as a famous guy, who deals
with that, being looked at—in his case, guarded at a restaurant, unable to go out for a beer," Bourdain said. "I asked
him very general questions to which he gave thoughtful, honest, reflective, and entertaining answers. I can't honestly say
there's any reason to expect that kind of experience with our
current president, who seems to have few interests beyond
himself. That's not interesting dinner company."

Bourdain has explored dozens of countries through the
four iterations of his show, but a few continue to elude him:
Venezuela ("We just can't get an insurance company to cover
us"), Afghanistan ("We keep trying"), Yemen ("The security
situation is impossible"), and Somalia. "They're all beautiful
countries with incredible stories other than conflict, terror-
ism and war," he said. As for North Korea: "I think under
current circumstances it would be in really poor taste to do
that," he said. "I mean, the people are starving. I do a food-
based show, ostensibly. If you see the hard news coverage,
you're so limited in what you're allowed to see. They create
a comfortable bubble for you at best; they clear everything.
We look for natural, authentic experience and that would be
impossible for us in North Korea."

CINEPHILE FOR LIFE

Bourdain said he spends more time in between shoots talking about movies with his crew. He cited a flurry of directors—Antonioni, Truffaut, Kurosawa, Fellini, Godard and Cassavetes—that he expected anyone working with him to know well. "I can't really even start a conversation unless you're already familiar with those guys," he said, adding that he also likes "great, trashy drive films from the '70s," particularly the ones directed by Peter Yates. "There's a baseline: Do you really like films? It's a requirement," he said. "With some directors, if you don't know them, it's weird."

Bourdain was raised in New Jersey in the '60s and '70s, when his father worked at a camera store in New York that had a rentable 16mm projector. "I grew up with really great films being shown in my house on weekends for family and a few friends," he said. "I'd probably seen the entire Janus Films collection by the time I was twelve. My parents were the sort of people who went to theaters to see Bergman and Antonioni. Filmmakers were respected in my house from the beginning." He delights in fusing his cinephilia with the design of the show: Anticipating the latest installment, his Buenos Aires episode is an explicit homage to Wong's *Happy Together*, while the editing style of the Paraguay episode was inspired by Steven Soderbergh's *The Limey*.

He also lists directors who are more obscure to Western audiences, such as Kinji Fukasaku and Shinya Tsukamoto, as key influences. "That's a fun part of making the show—getting to make small, cheap versions or homages to things that we love," he said.

Bourdain lives much of his life in transit, and watches a lot of movies when he's on the move. He rarely gets a chance to see new releases, though he did catch *Black Panther* during a stop in Nairobi. "It was a religious experience," he said. He tends to work through entire directors' filmographies. Recently, he said, he had been on a Bertolucci kick, until Argento insisted they focus on Pasolini. "When we're not shooting, we sit around talking about movies," he said.

Bourdain's relationship with Argento has overlapped with a dramatic chapter in her life, as the revelations about Weinstein's behavior included her own disclosures in Ronan Farrow's Pulitzer-winning story for the *New Yorker*. Argento endured traumatizing backlash from the media in her native Italy, and she fled the country as a result; she has been flinging a mixture of invective and messages of empowerment from her Twitter feed for months. "It's been a huge part of our life," Bourdain said. "As you can probably imagine, it's been very hard and continues to be very hard for Asia, but at the same time, it's inspiring. She's at the center of a conversation with a lot of women who want to share. That's something she takes really, really seriously."

Case in point: When Argento came to the Cannes Film Festival to present the best actress prize, she took the opportunity to call out the hypocrisy in the room. "In 1997, I was raped by Harvey Weinstein here at Cannes," she said. "This festival was his hunting ground . . . He will live in disgrace, shunned by a film community that once embraced him and covered up his crimes. And even tonight, sitting among you, there are those who still have to be held accountable for their conduct against women for behavior that does not belong in this industry." (Argento later tweeted that only Spike Lee congratulated her for her remarks.)

> This is the speech I wrote and spoke out loud tonight at Cannes. For all the brave women who came forward denouncing their predators, and for all the brave women who will come forward in the future. We got the power #metoo pic.twitter.com/ttJNipNFxR
> —Asia Argento (@AsiaArgento) May 19, 2018

Reflecting on the moment, Bourdain beamed. "From the second she said she'd been invited to present an award, I knew it would be a nuclear bomb," he said. "I was so proud of her. It was absolutely fearless to walk right into the lion's den and say what she said, the way she said it. It was an incredibly powerful moment, I thought. I am honored to know someone who has the strength and fearlessness to do something like that."

It doesn't take much to assert that Bourdain and Argento form a natural symbiosis: both radiate the aura of weathered cultural warriors, navigating a landscape that doesn't always know quite where to place them, even as it continues to respond to their moves. Considering the potential for this power couple leads one to the natural conclusion that the world needs less Kimye and more Bargento. "She listens to my advice and frequently if not most of the time, rejects it," said Bourdain, who released a throaty laugh that *almost* sounded like the tough guy might be welling up. "That is something that Asia cannot help but do," he said. "She is brutally honest about herself and anything, and it's a great quality."

ANTHONY BOURDAIN was born on June 25, 1956 in New York City, but raised in the nearby suburb of Leonia, New Jersey. His mother Gladys was a copy editor at *The New York Times*, and his father Pierre was an executive in the classical music recording industry. Bourdain said the spark for his culinary career came when, as a boy, he had his first oyster, while on a trip to France visiting his father's family. He would subsequently drop out of Vassar College to work in seafood restaurants in Provincetown, Massachusetts, then move on to attend the prestigious Culinary Institute of America. From there he worked at numerous restaurants in New York City, until landing at Brasserie Les Halles, where he rose to become executive chef. Later in life Bourdain was open about his extensive drug usage during these years. In the early 1990s, he published a couple of unsuccessful detective novels, but in 1999 he published an essay about restaurant life in the *New Yorker* magazine (called "Don't Eat Until You Read This") that would change his life. When an expanded version of the essay was published as a book called *Kitchen Confidential: Adventures in the Culinary Underbelly*, it became an immediate bestseller. Courted by producers to turn the book into a television show, Bourdain would go on to essentially create the food-travel show genre, hosting his own hugely popular programs: *A Cook's Tour*; *No Reservations*; and *Parts Unknown*. On June 8, 2018, Bourdain was on location filming an episode of *Parts Unknown* in Kaysersberg, France, when he was found dead in his hotel room, an apparent suicide.

HELEN ROSNER is the food correspondent for *The New Yorker* magazine, where she writes about gastronomic culture and history. Formerly, she was a cookbook editor at Workman Publishing; restaurant editor at *New York* magazine; executive editor at Eater.com; and executive digital editor at *Saveur* magazine. In 2016, she won the James Beard Foundation Journalism Award for her essay, "On Chicken Tenders."

JESSICA BENNETT is the former assistant editor of *Rain Taxi Review of Books* and founding editor of *Beacon Broadside*. She has written criticism, essays and interviews for *Publishers Weekly*, the *Ruminator Review*, and others.

JILL DUPLIEX is an Australian chef, critic, and food writer who is the author of numerous cookbooks. After a long stint as food editor of *The Times* (of London), she returned to Sydney, where she is a frequent guest on TV and radio, and writes regularly for leading publications including the *Sydney Morning Herald* and *The Age*.

NEIL DEGRASSE TYSON is an astrophysicist who is the director of the Hayden Planetarium in New York. He has served on government commissions related to the aerospace industry and space travel, and written for numerous popular publications on those issues. Tyson has hosted several of his own television and radio programs on PBS and National Geographic.

JOHN W. LITTLE is the creator of *Blogs of War* and the host of the *Covert Contact* national security podcast. His analysis and reporting related to encryption and intelligence collection has received global coverage from major news organizations, and he is a 2017 Institute for the Future fellow.

PETER ARMSTRONG is a long-time CBC News journalist, having served in many capacities there, including as Jerusalem bureau chief, anchor of CBC Radio's *World Report*, and as host of the business news series on CBC TV, *On the Money*.

TREVOR NOAH is a South African comedian and actor who is host of the satirical news television program *The Daily Show*. His 2016 autobiography, *Born a Crime*, was a critically acclaimed bestseller.

ERIC KOHN is executive editor and chief critic for Indiewire. His work has also appeared *The New York Times*, *New York* magazine, *Variety*, *Filmmaker*, and elsewhere.

THE LAST INTERVIEW SERIES

KURT VONNEGUT: THE LAST INTERVIEW

"I think it can be tremendously refreshing if a creator of literature has something on his mind other than the history of literature so far. Literature should not disappear up its own asshole, so to speak."

$15.95 / $17.95 CAN
978-1-61219-090-7
ebook: 978-1-61219-091-4

JACQUES DERRIDA: THE LAST INTERVIEW
LEARNING TO LIVE FINALLY

"I am at war with myself, it's true, you couldn't possibly know to what extent... I say contradictory things that are, we might say, in real tension; they are what construct me, make me live, and will make me die."

translated by PASCAL-ANNE BRAULT and MICHAEL NAAS

$15.95 / $17.95 CAN
978-1-61219-094-5
ebook: 978-1-61219-032-7

ROBERTO BOLAÑO: THE LAST INTERVIEW

"Posthumous: It sounds like the name of a Roman gladiator, an unconquered gladiator. At least that's what poor Posthumous would like to believe. It gives him courage."

translated by SYBIL PEREZ and others

$15.95 / $17.95 CAN
978-1-61219-095-2
ebook: 978-1-61219-033-4

THE LAST INTERVIEW SERIES

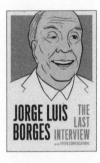

JORGE LUIS BORGES: THE LAST INTERVIEW

"Believe me: the benefits of blindness have been greatly exaggerated. If I could see, I would never leave the house, I'd stay indoors reading the many books that surround me."

translated by KIT MAUDE

$15.95 / $15.95 CAN
978-1-61219-204-8
ebook: 978-1-61219-205-5

HANNAH ARENDT: THE LAST INTERVIEW

"There are no dangerous thoughts for the simple reason that thinking itself is such a dangerous enterprise."

$15.95 / $15.95 CAN
978-1-61219-311-3
ebook: 978-1-61219-312-0

RAY BRADBURY: THE LAST INTERVIEW

"You don't have to destroy books to destroy a culture. Just get people to stop reading them."

$15.95 / $15.95 CAN
978-1-61219-421-9
ebook: 978-1-61219-422-6

THE LAST INTERVIEW SERIES

JAMES BALDWIN: THE LAST INTERVIEW

"You don't realize that you're intelligent until it gets you into trouble."

$15.95 / $15.95 CAN
978-1-61219-400-4
ebook: 978-1-61219-401-1

GABRIEL GÁRCIA MÁRQUEZ: THE LAST INTERVIEW

"The only thing the Nobel Prize is good for is not having to wait in line."

$15.95 / $15.95 CAN
978-1-61219-480-6
ebook: 978-1-61219-481-3

LOU REED: THE LAST INTERVIEW

"Hubert Selby. William Burroughs. Allen Ginsberg. Delmore Schwartz... I thought if you could do what those writers did and put it to drums and guitar, you'd have the greatest thing on earth."

$15.95 / $15.95 CAN
978-1-61219-478-3
ebook: 978-1-61219-479-0

THE LAST INTERVIEW SERIES

ERNEST HEMINGWAY: THE LAST INTERVIEW

"The most essential gift for a good writer is a built-in, shockproof shit detector."

$15.95 / $20.95 CAN
978-1-61219-522-3
ebook: 978-1-61219-523-0

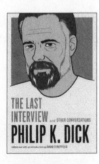

PHILIP K. DICK: THE LAST INTERVIEW

"The basic thing is, how frightened are you of chaos? And how happy are you with order?"

$15.95 / $20.95 CAN
978-1-61219-526-1
ebook: 978-1-61219-527-8

NORA EPHRON: THE LAST INTERVIEW

"You better *make* them care about what you think. It had better be quirky or perverse or thought-ful enough so that you hit some chord in them. Otherwise, it doesn't work."

$15.95 / $20.95 CAN
978-1-61219-524-7
ebook: 978-1-61219-525-4

THE LAST INTERVIEW SERIES

JANE JACOBS: THE LAST INTERVIEW

"I would like it to be understood that all our human economic achievements have been done by ordinary people, not by exceptionally educated people, or by elites, or by supernatural forces."

$15.95 / $20.95 CAN
978-1-61219-534-6
ebook: 978-1-61219-535-3

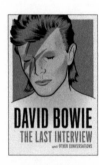

DAVID BOWIE: THE LAST INTERVIEW

"I have no time for glamour. It seems a ridiculous thing to strive for… A clean pair of shoes should serve quite well."

$16.99 / $22.99 CAN
978-1-61219-575-9
ebook: 978-1-61219-576-6

MARTIN LUTHER KING, JR.: THE LAST INTERVIEW

"Injustice anywhere is a threat to justice everywhere."

$15.99 / $21.99 CAN
978-1-61219-616-9
ebook: 978-1-61219-617-6

THE LAST INTERVIEW SERIES

CHRISTOPHER HITCHENS: THE LAST INTERVIEW

"If someone says I'm doing this out of faith, I say,
Why don't you do it out of conviction?"

$15.99 / $20.99 CAN
978-1-61219-672-5
ebook: 978-1-61219-673-2

HUNTER S. THOMPSON: THE LAST INTERVIEW

"I feel in the mood to write a long weird story–a tale
so strange and terrible that it will change the brain
of the normal reader forever."

$15.99 / $20.99 CAN
978-1-61219-693-0
ebook: 978-1-61219-694-7

DAVID FOSTER WALLACE: THE LAST INTERVIEW AND OTHER CONVERSATIONS

"I'm a typical American. Half of me is dying to give
myself away, and the other half is continually
rebelling."

$16.99 / 21.99 CAN
978-1-61219-741-8
ebook: 978-1-61219-742-5

THE LAST INTERVIEW SERIES

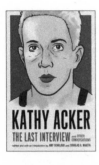

KATHY ACKER: THE LAST INTERVIEW AND OTHER CONVERSATIONS

"To my mind I was in a little cage in the zoo that instead of 'monkey' said 'female American radical.'"

$15.99 / $20.99 CAN
978-1-61219-731-9
ebook: 978-1-61219-732-6

PRINCE: THE LAST INTERVIEW AND OTHER CONVERSATIONS

"That's what you want. Transcendence. When that happens—oh, boy."

$16.99 / $22.99 CAN
978-1-61219-745-6
ebook: 978-1-61219-746-3

JULIA CHILD: THE LAST INTERVIEW AND OTHER CONVERSATIONS

"I'm not a chef, I'm a teacher and a cook."

$16.99 / $22.99 CAN
978-1-61219-733-3
ebook: 978-1-61219-734-0

THE LAST INTERVIEW SERIES

URSULA K. LE GUIN: THE LAST INTERVIEW AND OTHER CONVERSATIONS

"Resistance and change often begin in art.
Very often in our art, the art of words."

$16.99 / $21.99 CAN
978-1-61219-779-1
ebook: 978-1-61219-780-7